Moonflower

Moonflower: Defiantly Blooming in the Face of Great Darkness

Copyright © 2024 Sarah Beth Gerbers

All rights reserved. No part of this publication may be reproduced in a retrieval system, or transmitted in any form or by any means—electronic, mechanical, photocopying, recording, or otherwise—without the prior written permission of the publisher.

Unless otherwise noted, Scriptures are quoted in the English Standard Version® (ESV®) Copyright © 2001 by Crossway, a publishing ministry of Good News Publishers. All rights reserved. ESV Text Edition: 2016. Scriptures taken from the Holy Bible, New International Version®, NIV®. Copyright © 1973, 1978, 1984, 2011 by Biblica, Inc.™ Used by permission of Zondervan. All rights reserved worldwide. www.zondervan.com The "NIV" and "New International Version" are trademarks registered in the United States Patent and Trademark Office by Biblica, Inc.™.

Scripture quotations marked (NLT) are taken from the Holy Bible, New Living Translation, copyright ©1996, 2004, 2015 by Tyndale House Foundation. Used by permission of Tyndale House Publishers, Carol Stream, Illinois 60188. All rights reserved. Scripture quotations taken from the Berean Study Bible, BSB, Copyright ©2016, 2020 by Bible Hub. Used by Permission. All Rights Reserved Worldwide. https://bereanbible.com.

This book is set in the typeface *Athelas* designed by Veronika Burian and Jose Scaglione.

Original cover art and interior illustrations by Emily Person.

Paperback ISBN: 979-8-3294-4182-6
Hardcover ISBN: 979-8-3304-1283-9

A Publication of *Tall Pine Books*
www.tallpinebooks.com

| 1 22 22 20 16 02 |

Published in the United States of America

Moonflower

Defiantly Blooming in the Face of Great Darkness

Sarah Beth Gerbers

"Clarifying the obscure ache that lingers at the edges of your psyche, Sarah Gerbers puts words to the emotions we all feel. Defanging the darkness that haunts your soul, she illuminates the caverns that we all fall into, *with hope*. In *Moonflower*, you are invited into a journey through the soul-scorching seasons that Sarah's family has endured. With raw vulnerability and authenticity, she welcomes you into her multiple treks through the valley of the shadow of death. One thing will be clear as you read: Sarah knows the way through the darkest of nights."

DAN HEROD
Author of *The Three Mile Valley*

"*Moonflower*, indeed, transforms the immaterial, abstract concept of "hope" into a living, breathing artform readers can immediately pick up for themselves. *It did for me!* Gerbers' hard-earned outlooks of joy and gratitude for life, love, and all the small wonders is inspirational, contagious, and life-giving. Each chapter of her story will have you mining gems for your own path forward; hence, if you need a new lens on life to bloom in the darkness, *Moonflower* is your answer! Own this tender book because it will be a grounding go-to resource."

—ANGELA ATLAS
Author of *Moon Pedaler*

"Beautifully written...honest and full of raw emotion. Sarah's words will draw you in and captivate you with such inspiration to see beauty even in the most difficult of circumstances."

—SANDI BROWN
Christian novelist and founder of *Bridges of Hope*

"I am in awe reading Sarah's vulnerable and raw story of grief, pain, and suffering. She has a brilliant way of weaving words together into a beautiful masterpiece while, at the same time, writing so intimately that you feel like you're right across the coffee shop table with her. For all of us who have experienced a "dark night of the soul," *Moonflower* creates a safe space for you to feel seen, heard, and deeply understood. It is not only a work of art that you will want to highlight, underline, and savor for years to come, but you will walk away empowered to bloom amidst life's darkest moments."

—Kayla Cornish
Speaker, Writer, and Co-Founder of *Legacy Roots Co.*

"*Moonflower* drew me in from the very first page. I was touched by Sarah's poignant telling of her painful losses, as well as her honest wrestling with unanswerable questions. Sarah vulnerably reveals what it looks like to "defiantly bloom in the face of great darkness." Her journey towards open-handed trust and surrender invites each of us to consider our own losses, our own questions, our own wrestling and our own surrender.

Moonflower brims with hope, and I highly recommend this book to anyone who is struggling to make sense of their own losses. Sarah confidently reminds us that when we yield our lives to the Master Gardner, He is able to make beautiful flowers bloom even in seasons of darkness."

—Bev Roozeboom
Spiritual Director and Author of
Unlocking the Treasure and *A Day in the Life*

*For Kirk, Addie, and our five we have yet to meet.
Together, we are set apart for His glory.*

*I will defiantly bloom
in the face of great darkness.*

Contents

Introduction   xiii

1. Am I Drowning, or Am I Breathing?   1
   Part One   5
2. Broken Open   9
3. Again and Again and Again and Again   15
4. After   19
5. The Shadow Place   25
6. His Hand   31
7. Silencing Why   39
8. Loss is Loss is Loss   43
9. Frostbitten   49
10. The Patient Gardener   55
11. Spring Always Comes   59
12. Pressed Down   67
    Part Two   69
13. Soft and Slow   73
14. Tears   79
15. Amber Gems   87
16. The Power of a Name   91
17. Poison in the Bones   99
18. And She Heard the Birds   105
19. Songs of Deliverance   111
20. Upward   117
21. But Now I See   123
22. Unearthing Treasure   129
23. Pruning   135
    Part Three   139
24. Release   141
25. Open Hands   145
26. Surrender and Submission   151
27. Amy   159

28. A Gift	169
29. Fear and Anxiety	179
30. Let Go	189
31. Dancing in October	193
32. Rest is Surely Coming	199
Part Four	203
33. Joy Remains	205
34. Abide	209
35. This is Worship, Too	219
36. The Joy of Jesus	227
37. Delicate	233
38. He Provides	241
39. He Restores	249
40. Though Storms Will Come	257
41. An Invitation	265
Acknowledgments	267
Discussion Questions	271
About the Author	293
Notes	295
Index	297

Introduction

As the sun begins to sink low into its billowy bed at the close of a warm summer day, the moonflowers begin to awaken. Ivy leaves stretch up trellises as if lengthening into yawns, and as stars begin to unveil one by one, silky alabaster petals lift their faces to the glittering sky. Blooms unfurl into ivory trumpets as their spicy-sweet fragrance releases into the night air. An evening perfume, it is said, that captivates all who pass by.

While other flowers flourish in golden daylight, the moonflowers slumber. Like a whispered lullaby, they do not demand attention but subtly and subversively thrive under the cover of darkness. One must be awake and observant in the nighttime hours to feast on the moonflower's full, quiet beauty.

I first became aware of the moonflower on a drizzly summer evening while sitting on a red park bench overlooking a glass-mirrored pond. I had just received a piece of very troubling news, and I didn't know what to do. I was overwhelmed and hurting, and as I sat under the soft rain and darkening sky, something caught my attention. To my right, a collection of vines and white flowers stretched toward the sky. I walked over to the blooms and noticed their details. "What are these flowers?" I wondered to myself.

Then and there, I began researching on my phone. I read about the moonflowers' nature and learned how they are one of the nocturnal wonders of the botanical world. A flower that blooms in the night. How unique. I thought about the bad news I had just been given. I felt like I was entering a darkened night of my own. Immediately, I felt a nudge of comparison. Was it possible to learn something of value from these flowers?

As I watched these soft, milky petals open in the night, I thought about all the previous life experiences that showed me it is possible to grow through the darkness. Like the moonflower, I have learned to not merely live, but *thrive* in unlit, unexpected places. If I grew in difficult times before, perhaps I could do it again.

Through time, God has taught me what I previously could not see by using this example from His creation. I have cultivated and tended to my own moonflowers since this first encounter, and applicable lessons continue to be revealed through their unusual way of thriving. Consequently, I have learned to do the same.

Through the four sections of this book, we will journey through the moonflower's life cycle as it relates to us. I will speak honestly about the grief and loss that shatters our hearts into pieces. I will discuss the surprising ways we can flourish despite living inside the sticky textures of grief and brokenness. Together, we will discover it is possible to live with our hands and hearts wide open. We will shine a spotlight on stilling the chaos of life so we can discover the joy that lies beyond our limited expectations and the realities of ache.

I am hopeful my experiences will allow you to consider the losses, disappointments, and griefs you meet as unlikely invitations to live a richer, fuller life. Could it be, our most desolate circumstances can add exquisite meaning and wisdom to our souls? And is it true, our losses can open our eyes to the intricate beauty hidden in even the most mundane moments? Every season of our lives holds joy like precious blooms waiting to be discovered, even in the night, and even in places we think we could not possibly flourish.

While the purpose of my etchings is not to offer steps or formulas to perfectly heal as you imagine you should, they exist to become balm to a weary soul. My hope is you will come to know the "Great Gardener of Souls" who plants, prunes, and lovingly tends to our lives even when circumstances tell us He is not good. To thrive in the night like the moonflowers is to be a rebellious anomaly, and you're invited into such an experience. Are you willing to allow your eyes to adjust to the darkness? There are so many surprising details waiting there to be discovered.

This collection of stories, essays, and poems is an exposed piece of my heart. It is worship written for the complete honor of God. It is my offering, like incense arising from ash. I have walked through five miscarriages and losses of many kinds, but even when my limited intellect would suggest otherwise, He has never left my side. I desire to be vulnerable because I refuse to let my difficulties go to waste. I am allowing both my weaknesses and lessons learned to be a reminder for you: God is ever-present among all life's circumstances and cares. It is important to share all the difficult pieces of life because it all matters. Even though this story of mine begins with much heaviness, He has come alongside to make my burden ever so light.

My story is not entirely unique. An assortment of people have lived situations similar to mine, and many are well acquainted with the textures of grief. In fact, if you are alive and breathing, you will face trials of many kinds. So here I am, a

Introduction

fellow traveler in this world of various experiences, grasping onto your hand and pointing up at the evening sky to say, "Look! There's so much beauty here. You are not alone, and we are traveling this wondrous and complex life together. You and I can thrive here, even in the night."

Chapter 1

Am I Drowning, or Am I Breathing?

On the cusp of an ordinary weekday morning, I startled awake while gasping for air. "What a wild dream," I thought as I pulled myself from bed. I tiptoed into our teenage daughter's bedroom with our dog trailing closely behind me. We were her faithful wake-up committee, and it was time to begin a new day. "Addie," I whispered, "it's time to get up."

Soon all three of us shuffled into the bathroom together, and as I ran the brush through Addie's long, tangled hair, she looked at my reflection in the mirror and said, "Mom, you woke me out of the weirdest dream."

"I had a crazy dream this morning, too," I said. "You go first. Tell me yours." Addie rubbed her sleepy eyes and began to explain. "I was standing at the edge of a pool, and someone came from behind me to wrap their arms around me. I couldn't move at all. Whoever it was threw me into the pool, but they went with me and kept hugging me tightly. The person felt like a weight.

"We kept sinking deeper, and it was like there was no bottom to the pool. I was trying so hard to break free and get to the surface, but I had no control. I couldn't hold my breath anymore and I thought I would drown. I mean, I didn't expect I would even be going into the pool in the first place, so I didn't even take a deep breath before we went into the water. But after a while, I really couldn't stop myself from opening my mouth to swallow the water. I knew I was going to drown. Then—it was so weird—I started to breathe underwater. The arms of the person were still wrapped around me and I was still sinking deeper, but I could breathe.

"Even though I should have been scared, I wasn't. It was so dark and there was no sound, but I wasn't afraid anymore. It was actually pretty peaceful. I don't think the person behind me was trying to drown me, but only wanted to show me I could breathe underwater. I wouldn't have known that had I not been thrown into the pool."

As she told me the story of her dream, my brush strokes ceased. I could do nothing but stare at her reflection with my mouth wide open. "Addie," I marveled, "I had the exact same dream. I woke up from it right before I came into your room to begin the day."

We both looked at each silently for a moment, trying to understand.

"So you breathed under the water in your dream, too? Someone grabbed you from behind and sank you down into the water?" she asked.

"Word for word. What you just told me of your dream was the exact same dream I just had," I replied.

"What do you think this means?"

"I have no idea. I'm going to have to think about it for a bit. I usually don't try to figure out if my dreams mean anything, but the simple fact that we both had the same dream at basically the same time is definitely REALLY weird," I answered.

I still don't know exactly why my daughter and I had identical dreams on the same early morning, and quite honestly, it still boggles my mind. We never experienced such a thing in the past, and we haven't since. However, as I considered the details of our dreams, I see a possible reason behind them.

My very best attempt at interpretation is this: the person who pulled us into the water might have been God. Neither Addie nor I were actively going into the pool by ourselves, and as we stood at the water's edge, it didn't seem to be in our thoughts to jump in. I assume we wouldn't have experienced the water on our own accord, so God scooped His mighty arms around us and plunged us into the depths. The water was dark, deep, and quite uncomfortable, but He did not leave us. We struggled with all our might to break free and swim to the surface on our own, but we did not have enough strength to do so. Even though we continued to sink, we discovered firsthand that survival could be found in such a situation. We thought we would drown, but instead we realized we could breathe where it would rationally be impossible. We took breaths in the depths of the water and realized we were not alone. We wouldn't have been in that situation had it not been for the strong arms pulling us to the depths, but we would have never experienced the miracle of breathing instead of drowning if the Someone behind us had not shown us such a wonder.

Both Addie and I woke up before we could see any resolution to our dreams. We never turned around to see who was with us in the water, and we could not stay long enough to see if we ever floated up to the surface to take a gulp of oxygen. Maybe we didn't need to. Perhaps a full resolution was not even necessary. We already knew we were okay simply because those secure arms were holding us.

And we could breathe.

Later that day, Addie and I discussed the fact that if our dreams meant anything, it might be all of this. She nodded her head in complete agreement. I already knew what it was like to breathe in the depths, and perhaps God was revealing this knowledge to my daughter, as well. As a very little girl, she witnessed our struggles and watched as we began to breathe among what seemed like suffocation. She was there when we realized we could survive in the dark, watery night. This lesson is for her. It is for me. *It is for all of us.*

Part One
Seed

our deepest needs
our fractured places
our splintered pieces
are holy spaces
Your tender love
reaches, fills,
binds and suffuses

Chapter 2

Broken Open

A minuscule, hard-shelled seed held in a gardener's palm holds a world of value in its belly. Of course, the seed could sit for years comfortably remaining the same, but it would never become what it is supposed to be while unused and unplanted. The seed does not exist to be wasted in this manner because it was created to flourish into its fullest potential. But in order to do this, it must first be made uncomfortable.

Since the moonflower seed has an extremely tough exterior, gardeners must pierce the outer shell and soak it in water prior to the planting process. While this step could be skipped over, both piercing and soaking give the best opportunity for future strength and growth. As the cracked-open shell is softened and moisture begins to infiltrate the wound, the seed experiences its first chance at life.

If we were able to ask the seed how this rude awakening feels, it would likely describe it as a painful and confusing violation. We can imagine any experience that includes stabbing and drowning would feel much more like death than life. Pulled from the comforts of simply "being," it is thrust into what seems much like an ending. However, for the moonflower to have the best chance to reach its full potential, it must endure this step even prior to being pressed into the soil. This is where its life is initiated. Before wide open petals emerge in the lush warmth of late summer, breaking and immersing must occur in early spring.

On a chilly April Sunday morning, I found myself suddenly cracked wide open and thrust into a situation that felt as if it was designed to destroy. When you are the one in this "moonflower seed" situation, it is incredibly difficult to imagine something beautiful eventually resulting from such brokenness. In fact, as I found myself in the church bathroom stall with blood rolling down my legs a mere fifteen minutes before I was supposed to be onstage leading our congregation in worship, beauty was far from my thoughts. Just a few weeks prior, we learned I was pregnant with our second child. The joy and excitement of this news gave way to complete disappointment in the blink of an eye.

Our first pregnancy had been a difficult one, as we came close to losing our sweet Addie on a few different occasions while she grew in my belly. I knew the dizzying feeling of holding my breath while life stitched together in my womb. I understood the risks. What an experience it is to carry life in your core, yet hold very little say as to how the cells involved join together into a puzzle-piece work of art. With Addie, we experienced the miraculous when she was born both full-term and wonderfully healthy.

But as I watched blood drops hit the tan tiled floor that April Sunday morning, I knew this second pregnancy was quite opposite. No one had to explain to me what was happening. It was blatantly obvious this fresh new life was leaving my body. The puzzle pieces were falling apart, and all alone in that cold bathroom, I was very suddenly saying goodbye to someone I would never have the privilege of knowing.

I wept as I cleaned away the drops of what could have been. In that moment, a reality ripped through my heart: while I was due to lead a congregation in worship (and could only wonder what the full presence of God entails), our baby was already experiencing heaven in full. My own flesh and blood was already there. While this had the potential to be a comforting thought, no parent wishes for their child to reach heaven before them. I felt betrayed by the God I was about to worship. How could I even think about singing the words, "You give and take away, blessed be Your name," with heartfelt authenticity while actively losing a child? I was certain He was permitting this life to be taken away, so how could this possibly be good? How could HE possibly be good?

I gathered myself together in front of the bathroom mirror and wiped away my smeared makeup. There was nobody else there that day to lead worship, so it was up to me. Even though my life had just been entirely altered, I pasted an ordinary facade across my face. Nobody could know about this quite yet. I had to first lead worship and pretend like I meant it.

Robotically, I went through the motions of ministry on that early spring morning. As life left my body, my mouth uttered empty words to God. As waves of pain rolled through, I put on the academy award performance of praise. I refused to permit any possible unraveling process to take place while other eyes were upon me. I was one of their leaders, and vulnerably placing myself in the hands of their inevitable pity was an uncomfortable thought. I believed I was supposed to be strong and "put together" as a picture of pretend pastoral perfection. It wasn't until I arrived home that I melted into my husband's arms. Prior to that day, miscarriage was something that happened to other people. Now it was happening to us, and it was completely awful. It felt like a terrible injustice.

Since our loss was early, the physical healing process was fairly fast. In fact, the doctors suggested waiting only a month before entertaining the idea of pregnancy once again. However, the emotional impact of miscarriage reaches deeper than flesh, bone, and time itself. I felt a litany of emotions cracking fractures throughout my soul in the form of crippling fear, confusion, anger, emptiness, loneliness, sadness, and depression (among so many other things). "Beauty from ashes" requires both tenacious effort and abiding patience, and sometimes circumstances feel far too debilitating to consider either. The emotions tied to sorrow are entirely strong. The "healing process" is a current that takes agreement to wade into, and I was not ready to dip my toes into such water. I was grieving, and grief has a habit of staying with no perceivable timeline. In fact, grief changes everything forever and it can cause one to question the very capability of God.

That spring Sunday marked me forever. It is the day we lost a child for the first time. I think of those arms pulling me under the water in my dream and how I flailed and fought all the way down. I did not choose this. Never in a million years would I have picked this story to be added to the anthology of my life. It was far too uncomfortable and entirely too painful to ever be desired.

Little moonflower seed, I suppose this is what it feels like to be cracked open and submerged. It is a confusing injury to hurt so deeply, but to still keep living.

all the oxygen exited my lungs
in a fierce and brutal blow

for a moment I could not
find another breath
as I kept sinking, sinking
in undiluted blue

deeper, deeper the anvil pulled

I opened my mouth
as water licked the walls of my lungs
"so this is the taste of drowning"
I thought to myself

but instead of choking on liquid steel
I drank in a crisp gulp of something new

I found Him there
in the depths of deep blue

with a brave, full breath I asked,
"Can I breathe here, too?"

Chapter 3

Again and Again and Again and Again

Do not let anyone tell you that you faced tragedy because your faith was not large enough. Don't speak such a thing to yourself, either. Because sometimes you can muster up the largest measure of human-made faith and your prayers do not unfold to reveal your desired result tucked neatly inside. Sometimes you pray all the words, do the right things, follow the advice, and have all the faith, but your will for your own life continues to unravel to reveal a host of undesired experiences. How do I know this?

I became pregnant again, and we had to say goodbye.

And then again.

And again.

And again.

In all, five little ones slipped out of reach and there was nothing I could do. I desperately tried everything placed within my reach to change my circumstances and receive different results. I took all the medications, endured treatments, became a human test subject, and was stuck with seemingly thousands of needles. More importantly, I prayed ceaselessly while firmly believing in God's ability to heal whatever was amiss in both mine and our babies' bodies, but I did not experience the healing I desired.

Sometimes we can have all the faith in the world but not see our miracles displayed as we wish. Faith, after all, cannot be placed upon measuring sticks. It certainly isn't quantified by how many times we get what we have desired, prayed for, or demanded. Faith is not magic. It is an enduring resolve to believe God is good even when we are not granted what we have believed would be ours.

I invited anger
over for dinner
and we lingered for a while
getting to know each other

after time had passed
and the moon had risen
anger confided,
"my real name is sorrow.
I simply require
your attention."*

---

* "I sat with my anger long enough until she told me her real name was grief." C.S. Lewis

Chapter 4

After

Here is what life is often like after miscarriage: You feel guilty, as though your own body betrayed you. The life you were supposed to shelter did not find provision under your care. Even though you know you did all you could, it was not enough; and for this you feel responsible. You awaken in the middle of the night clutching your stomach to feel for a life that is no longer there. Before your eyes fully open, you forget for just a moment, but then it all comes rushing back like a wall of thick waves. Waking up from slumber's respite means becoming drenched in the reality of sorrow all over again. There seems to be an empty place inside of your core—a carved-out canyon, a bottomless gorge.

You receive kind condolences mixed with a collection of confusing words. "Maybe God is telling you that you should adopt," says one lady. Another person concludes, "Maybe God knew your children weren't going to follow Him later in life, so He chose to take them now to secure their salvation." What? "What am I supposed to do with these opinions?" you wonder.

You realize people mean well, but you have a hard time receiving the myriads of phrases and pieces of advice. This is

After

something that happens to other people, after all. It is not supposed to happen to you. But it did, and now you are at the receiving end of a ringing doorbell as someone hands you a casserole. A friend brings flowers. Your sister sends a basket of fruit. You accept the gifts, read the cards, and hear the words, but everyone else goes back to living and you are left pushing casserole around your plate while sitting in the dark. The world keeps turning, but you are stuck in the night. You are the only one who feels the deep textures of such a loss, the only one who feels the empty space.

There are no funerals or memorial services. No one holds memories containing this nameless person who once shared your body. You keep record of would-be due dates and note places on the calendar that could have been filled with celebration and cake. You miss the pictures never taken, the kisses never given, and even the sleepless nights you could have spent rocking a restless bundle of life. It is a loss as deep as any other, but there is no closure.

You think there should be funerals for miscarriages even if you are the one who says all the words. You are this baby's mother and you will advocate for its importance even though the time on earth was so very brief. This human was important and deserves to be remembered by the whole world, you think. This baby boy, or baby girl, did not have to become something greater to matter. You felt its existence and that was enough to mark your life forever. Yes, you will write the words and sing the songs to give your baby the funeral that should be.

But this does not happen, and you are instead left looking in the rearview mirror, wondering what it would have been like to see another car seat perched in the backseat. You put away the baby clothes and take the crib back into the basement. You wonder if you will ever unpack these boxes again.

For the rest of your life, you will wonder at the memories never made. You will continue to imagine what it would have been like if you did not have to say goodbye. As long as you are alive, there will not be a single moment you stop missing your child. You will always feel the empty space and the textures of the ache. You will always feel the anger over what was seemingly snatched from your hands. This is how it is. This is what it is often like after life leaves your womb.

my hands must be emptied
to feel the textures of Your fingerprints
against mine
for if I am holding onto everything
except You
I have nothing at all

Chapter 5

The Shadow Place

After honestly writing years' worth of painful lament to God on paper not too long ago, I set down my pen and stared blankly at the woods situated just outside my window. Nearly a decade and a half later, I still find myself in mourning. Flares of anger toward God keep flashing to the surface of my soul.

"Are you finished?" I felt God inquire to my soul. "If so, I would really like to meet with you. Put on your boots and come outside."

As thin clouds laced over the sun, I listened to the early spring snow crunch underfoot. The cool breeze slipped through tall pines and then came near, brushing through strands of my hair. There in the hush, I heard God's whisper. "I promised in My Word you will have trouble here. You will have grief because this world is not equipped for eternity. There will be reason to lament over and over again because everything here is temporary and will leave your hands. Everything except for Me. The only thing you can grip tightly to and never lose is ME. You're not alone, and you never were, because I have promised to never leave. *Stop expecting a temporary world to be eternal. Stop expecting a temporary world to give you what can only be afforded in eternity."* Wow. Okay, God, I am listening.

I thought about how my family and I have been thrust into lament over and over again. I replayed in my mind all the times I expected the temporary to stay in the here and now with certainty. I began to painfully recall how several months after our first miscarriage, we learned we were expecting again. Because of our previous loss, my doctor kept a very close eye on the progress of my pregnancy. I was sent to the hospital for frequent blood work panels and ultrasounds, and at first, everything appeared to be moving in the right direction. I was thankful and confident. I believed deep in my heart God was going to allow this child to thrive. Certainly, He would not ask us to go through the experience of miscarriage again.

I will never forget the phone call that rearranged everything. During an ordinary day filled with ordinary things, another imperfect situation was cast upon us. On the other end of the phone, I heard my doctor say, "Sarah, I am so sorry. Your HCG levels are dropping at a steep rate, and you will be miscarrying again. You might want to prepare yourself because your body will be responding shortly. Please call us when it does, and we will guide you to the next steps."

I refused to accept the words he was saying. We asked our friends and family to pray ceaselessly alongside us for our unborn baby. God is more than capable of healing, and we believed if we pounded the gates of heaven with our prayers, He would surely answer our pleas in the way we desired. The Bible states we need only faith the size of a tiny mustard seed, and we certainly had enough to pack our fists full and overflowing as we petitioned this request before God. We prayed for a few days, and no sign of miscarriage arrived. We were more than certain He was graciously answering our prayer.

While undergoing an ultrasound the next week, the worst was realized. There was no sign of a fluttering little heartbeat found in our baby's body. Another brief life had slipped away while we were praying and believing for the opposite to occur. We couldn't keep this baby either. While we sat across from my doctor as he was carefully explaining the options for "taking care of the baby's body," I cupped my head in my hands and wept. I recall him comforting us the best he could, saying, "It is miraculous anyone is born healthy. If you think about all the millions of events that must perfectly take place as a baby is developing, it is a miracle anyone is born without complication. While you lost another baby, your daughter is a miracle." He was definitely right, but I deeply mourned the fact that God had not allowed our second and third babies to survive.

I was given the option of either a DNC surgery to remove our baby or a new medication that would supposedly help my body expel everything at home. The latter option was less invasive, they explained, and would carry no risk of leaving behind scar tissue that could complicate future pregnancies. We chose to take the medication and promptly went home. Little did we know, I was about to experience a taste of hell on earth.

After swallowing the medication, I felt as though I had been stabbed in the abdomen repeatedly by a sharp knife. I was instructed to take the pills not once, but three grueling times. Not only did I become incredibly ill, but I was also hemorrhaging an alarming amount. I was confined to the bathroom, unable to leave. As I laid weak and faint on the floor, I felt as if I was enduring a taste of death myself. Later that evening, I held our little baby's body in the palm of my hand. So very tiny. All this pain and drama was because of this little one we could never know here on earth. It felt so cruel, as if I were literally holding shattered pieces of my heart in my hands.

Since it was a Friday evening and the labs were closed for the weekend, the doctor's office instructed me to keep the baby in a "preserved state" until Monday morning. They wanted to test the baby's cells to see if they could find a cause for the failed pregnancy. Our little beloved baby's body had to sit in a cup of water in our refrigerator for the entire weekend while I continued to lay sick on the bathroom floor. On Monday morning, with young Addie strapped in the backseat of our car, we brought the precious cup containing her little sibling to the lab. So much trauma, but no cause would ever be found.

I laid in bed for days, shades pulled tight. Once again, much like the dream Addie and I had, I felt like I was sinking into deep, suffocating water. The outside light was denied permission to enter by the thick, confusing shadow of grief. My pillow became a tear-soaked sponge. All the pain and questions I became well acquainted with during our first miscarriage came racing back with increased intensity. I wondered how God could be good when He seemed to completely ignore our voices advocating for our little ones. I felt unseen, forgotten, and unloved by the God who was supposed to care. Loneliness crept from my empty womb and soaked deep into my bones.

One afternoon, as I continued to cover myself in a blanket of sorrow (refusing all phone calls, messages, and daily tasks), I distinctly felt the Holy Spirit fill the bedroom. This was the shadow place, and He was there. He was not afraid of it.

I have read about God being light and I assumed anywhere He is, there is no chance the shadows can survive. But that day, His tender Spirit came into the darkness and laid by my side. My sadness, anger, and pain were not chased away, nor was my situation remedied, but He was simply there abiding next to me. My anger did not send Him away and my tears did not make Him uncomfortable. My blaming questions didn't tear a hole in His character and my accusations did not redefine any aspect of His goodness. God was just simply and undeniably there.

At first, I could not hear His voice. Sometimes, if God seems silent, it doesn't mean He has left or has stopped speaking. Silence only means He is waiting to be found beyond the limits of words. What is felt is deeper than words, after all, and my shadow place was not off limits to discovering this. It wasn't until days later I FELT Him whisper, "Get up. Don't stay here. I know this hurts so much, but you're not meant to reside forever in this ache." I cannot articulate how I knew He was saying this without spoken words. There in the darkness, I simply sensed it.

Sometimes we are not broken just once, but multiple times over. The phrase, "God does not give us more than we can handle," is not found in the pages of our Bible, and it certainly is not true. Oftentimes this flawed life generously dishes out heaping portions we cannot handle on our own, but we are not meant to face any of it without God. *"Stop expecting a temporary world to be eternal. Stop expecting a temporary world to give you what can only be afforded in eternity,"* He said to me that day as I walked in the woods while painfully recalling a decade and a half of wounds. Oh my, does this life ache at times, but perhaps my expectations have been based upon that which is constantly shifting, and that which is not mine.

dusk exhales
and widens soft arms
to gather last light
and sweep away
final traces of day

as memories
of brilliant hues
are traded for
the deep twilight of blue
I wonder if I could learn
how to say goodbye
in such a beautiful way, too

Chapter 6

His Hand

There was a time I wished programs were in existence to offer uniform success in helping us find healing after seasons of pain. I spent many hours reading through stacks of resources just for that reason. I wanted an easy, tried-and-true solution to dissolve my grief as quickly as possible. Maybe it could be like diet programs—just like melting away pounds, perhaps it was possible shave off grief. I read books explaining how to mend broken hearts with swift efficiency. I ingested countless pieces of advice from well-meaning people describing how healing could be found in the same ways they discovered. I feverishly took notes while listening to various sermons and podcasts. Nothing seemed to work against the power of my grief.

With time, I came to the realization man-made programs fall short in successfully bringing all of us to a place of perfect mending. The magic glue that pulled someone else's broken pieces back together proved to be completely useless with my own. Others can explain how they managed to tame grief's feral ways while giving inspiring quotes and shouting cheers about "continuing on," but everyone's experiences are filled with unique curves and turns. Just as each of our fingertips contain mazes of individualistic prints, and just as the strands of DNA that stitch us together are unique, the ways in which we process sorrow are not at all uniform.

Grief is not one stand-alone occasion. Loss does not just come to visit once and vanish like vapor in air. Instead, pain washes back and forth, receding only to rise again. It sews threads deep into our veins. It stamps itself into the permanency of memory and holds no written timeline. While we can lovingly assist one another through tangled webs of heartbreak, it is not enough. It is humanly impossible for us to entirely heal one another. Our books, programs, and advice might soothe, but they alone do not bring forever-cures to the wounding this life can dish out.

As I discovered this over time, I began to inquire, "What if these one-size-fits-all programs lack uniform success because God is desiring to meet with us as individuals along the road of lament? What if, inch by inch, we might begin a unique journey to knowing Him more? What if it is not as much about healing but instead unearthing hidden truths? What if it is not about restoring back to factory settings but becoming entirely new? If all I sense in the darkness is not advice and man-made solutions, but only the hand of God reaching out for me, is that enough?"

I truly entertained these questions after the first three of our five miscarriages. On a Sunday evening, I was singing on the worship team at the church my husband and I were youth pastoring in Michigan. I was tired and worn down from what was quite literally a silent, barren season of loss. I was taking one active step at a time to not remain cocooned in bed… to "not stay there," but I was weary and lacking. While I knew in my mind God's presence was my help, and even felt Him come near in painful moments, I was struggling. All my questions remained unanswered and my pain was raw and unresolved. I sang worship songs from a platform that evening, but He seemed a million miles away. My words felt empty, as if the meaning was hollowed out. Even if God was speaking to me, my ears were too muffled by grief to hear. Was He truly far off? Had He turned His ear away from the sound of my voice, or was it I who allowed impenetrable walls to surround? I wondered all of this while my lungs pushed out songs dedicated to His praise.

I haven't had many "visions" in my life, but as I wearily led worship for our congregation that evening, I slipped into what I can only describe as such. As I closed my eyes and allowed hollow lyrics to drain from my lips, it was as if a scene was painted on the inside of my eyelids.

In the darkness, I saw a light winking in the distance. As I stepped forward, I squinted and realized the light was actually Jesus walking in front of me. I saw only His back at first, but I knew it was Him because He was light itself. No outside source was illuminating Him; light simply originated from within His being. There was only surrounding darkness and this stark, glimmering contrast of luminance.

As I drew near, Jesus ceased His steps forward. He turned around to face me, and without words, simply stretched out His hand while nodding for me to grab ahold. He smiled, and I laced my hand in His. We kept walking in the darkness, but I was *with* Him. Soon enough, we began walking into a fog so thick I couldn't even see Him next to me but could only feel His fingers pressed against mine.

There in the foggy, ashy darkness, Jesus began to laugh. A deep, guttural, beautiful laugh. A contagious laugh. I somehow sensed the sound of His laughter was not directed AT me, as if to mock my circumstances, but existed as assurance. Although I could not see anything, I felt His hand and heard His joy. His laughter seemed to say, "I'm with you, and I know what's ahead. The night may be thick now, but I know the way. You can trust with joy because I am good. Just stay with Me. Keep holding My hand. You won't stay here." All this was gleaned from the mere sound of His laughter dancing through the darkness.

I opened my eyes, and the vision was over just as quickly as it came. I was still on the platform singing, not having missed a beat. I was still hurting, and my lament was not erased, but I felt as if I had been given a gift. God had once again reminded me that He indeed was near. Yes, it was dark, but He hadn't gone anywhere. This was the same truth I felt when I sensed the Holy Spirit enter my bedroom after our second miscarriage, and this vision was a reminder of that moment He came near to me in the darkness of my pain. He didn't even need to speak, for His laughter sang more truth than I knew how to fully process. He knew what was ahead and was unafraid. He had never abandoned me in my affliction. Instead, He was simply there with an extended hand.

Perhaps I did not need man-made programs, self-help books, or podcasts to bring a healing strategy or a resolve to pain. In fact, maybe lament never dissolves but only changes. Maybe God wanted to meet me in the darkness with an invitation for me to lace my hand into His, laughter mingling with pain and piercing through the fog when nothing else could be perceived. There, walking with Him, is everything I need.

This vision—this gift—was a cornerstone on which to rebuild. Now it was up to me: would I continue to doubt God's ability to be God, or would I believe everything I knew about Him to be actual truth? Would I walk with Him even when I couldn't hear Him speak? Would I hold onto Him when I could not see? Would I trust even though life stung? It is one thing to read in His Word that He is with me and will never leave, but it's another to experience it. I decided I wanted to believe He is who He says He is, even in the mess of grief. If He indeed is all He claims to be, then He is big enough for my questions, my doubts, my pain, and my anger. He found me in the darkness time and time again, after all.

So I took His hand.

God is not interested in rebuilding shacks when He has blueprints for castles. Loss and pain are the consuming fires that burn former structures to the ground, and no mass-produced self-help books can help to gather charred pieces in order to put everything back together as it was before. Well-intended advice is not capable of extinguishing embers still smoldering in piles of rubble. But taking His hand? That could become transformational. He is with us in the wastelands. He is near in the dark. And all we need are His fingers laced in ours, and inch by inch, we can move forward together. Brick by brick, castles can be built upon the same ground tragedies once smoldered.

In the vision God gave me that evening on the platform, He laughed while extending to me His hand, and that was the start. He was near, and that could be enough if I chose. This is not where my life began falling back into its former order as I wished it should. Instead, this is where my eyes began to open as if beginning to truly see life for the very first time. This is where my thought processes began to entirely rearrange. This is where my ruin could transform into holy ground. This was the preparation of soil—the tilling of ground—so that cracked seed could be planted and have a chance at "more."

oh resilient one,
keep rebuilding
from ruins
no matter how
many times
your soul
has been
burned down
to the ground

dig deeper
past soil
cracking like dust
in your tired hands
yes, keep turning
the decayed earth
of your worn soul
just an inch deeper
there is something
capable of reaping
nourishment and light
sweet soil
in which fragrant blooms
can root and grow
despite frost and chill
and layers of night
keep tilling
until you uncover
a remnant of sticky sweet life
from which hope can
and will
seed and swell

Chapter 7

Silencing Why

I have tasted the word "why" over a million times. I have rolled those three letters around in my mouth, holding them on my tongue as their flavors sank in. I have bitterly spat them out, only to pick them up and toss them back into my mouth repeatedly. What an unwise decision, like chewing used gum from the sidewalk or continually sipping old, burned coffee riddled with grit. While "why" can be very beneficial, the context in which I have come to know this portion of its flavors has allowed me to discover it can also be entirely unfulfilling. Tainted by circumstance, it can be sour and bland both at once, complexity and confusion embodied in one unfulfilling taste.

On a starless night many years after feeling the first stings of loss, "why" once again crawled up from my heart and sat inside my mouth. Even though I am in this constant state of learning the lessons loss brings, this pesky question never seems to leave me alone. I continue to take God's hand every day, but I still desire explanations. I still turn to Him and ask (or beg, yell, and SCREAM), "WHY?!"

I tasted the familiar question again before tossing it upward into the clouds; and with warm, salty tears wetting my cheeks, I

Silencing Why

asked it once again. There was no answer, as usual. Only silence.

I might always be familiar with these particular empty flavors of "why," but that evening as the clouds deflected my question, I wondered this: even if God gave me answers for why He allowed five of our babies to die, and even if He clarified reasons for taking loved ones before my opinion of when their time should be, would any explanation be good enough for me?

"Why" would never change the past, alter timelines, nor raise the dead; and truly, there is no conceivable reasoning that could satisfy and silence my wondering. In my selfishness, God could explain with extreme profundity something such as, "I took them to save the entire world," and I would still desire my loved one to be back by my side instead. I would still rather hold our own babies in my arms. They were MY world, after all. For as many times as I have tossed the question of "why" toward God, maybe silence has been the only response because I have not had the capacity to accept anything else. In my temporary, limited view of the here and now, I have not had the eyesight for a grander portrait.

After years of demanding suitable answers from God, I paused amidst my expectations. For the first time, I realized perhaps explanations were not what I actually needed. Instead, a pivotal concept emerged: what if I CHOSE to spit the word "why" into God's hand and leave it there? How subversive it would be to cease the madness of demanding the right to know reasons behind what was outside of my control. In requiring explanations, I had still been striving to claim some sort of authority through perfect understanding. Maybe this action of spitting out "why" and leaving it there was part of the definition of trust. In exchange for the silence following "why," perhaps I could begin to taste other questions capable of producing more satisfying flavors, such as, "How can I use this to better understand life?" or "How can God meet me here as my comforter in my sorrow?"

That evening, silently crying in the dark, I tossed out "why" and then left it hanging in the vast expanse of His hand. I finally prayed, "God, I have a hard time believing my pain is a part of Your original plan, but this world is fractured by sin and death. I want to understand how You can truly be the comforter You say You are. Would You show me? I don't want to remain bitter because it hurts too much to live this way. Would You open my eyes to the sweet that must be hidden here? I have been prone to the negative and haven't believed You are working all things together for my good. Would You turn my eyes toward truth? Can You help me use my lament to find a greater measure of You? I can feel Your hand, but help me to sense it at every moment. Help me leave my questions here even if they're never answered. Help me to find Your presence instead of the resolutions I have demanded."

While it may not be realistic to entirely ignore the word "why" in association with loss (because I am flawed and so very human, prone to frequent backpedaling), leaving its demands in the hands of God was, and is, quite freeing. It means looking past all the "whys" and focusing upon the glorious "Who." And this "Who" is willing to reveal what is beyond temporary pain and accusatory questions.

I will never have the answers I have longed for, but I suppose I do not need them. They would never be good enough for me, anyhow. I am sure of this, however: my wounds may remain open until I die, but I will not enter heaven in a wounded state. This pain has an expiration date. Until then, I can either rot in my cyclical "whys" or trust in the One who is holding the authoring pen. This is trust—giving up the need for explanations I would deem unsatisfactory in exchange for the greater satisfaction of knowing a deeper measure of God.

perhaps if I stopped
wielding questions
as fiery weapons

stilled my tongue
quieted my mind
hushed my heart

I would realize
a lack of answers
does not mean
I am forgotten
unheard
alone
or punishable
it simply reveals
I am asking
the wrong questions
demanding
the wrong things

(can I know more of You here
where my empty questions
forever remain
in Your hands?)

Chapter 8

Loss is Loss is Loss

Once upon a time, I had a friend who gave birth to a beautiful baby boy. He entered the world in a blaze of bravery, defying odds and boldly surviving despite professional predictions. He was not perfectly well, but he was strong and beautiful. It was as if all the love in the entire universe was lavished upon him. Parents, grandparents, older sister, and anyone in the general vicinity of his gravitational pull showered him with endless affection. The simple fact he was here and breathing was a stunning miracle, and everyone wanted to savor him for as long as he could stay.

After his first few months of life, this sweet little boy began to struggle with his health. Doctor visits filled the calendar, and difficult news began to gather like clouds above their heads. Soon everything began to escalate like an avalanche of disappointment. Medical equipment, trial treatments, sleepless nights, hospital stays, fear and worry collected and compiled until one dim day, the hopes and dreams held for this loved, little boy were snuffed away. "He has one month to live," the doctors declared.

Although he was only a half of a year old, his family acted

in the most beautiful display of love. They celebrated a collection of holidays in his final four weeks on earth. After putting up the Christmas tree, they gave each other beautiful gifts in the middle of summer surrounded by glowing holiday lights. They dressed up for Halloween, hid Easter eggs, and lit fireworks and sparklers while sharing a barbecued feast. They sang many "happy birthdays" while devouring delicious cake just so they could be together with him to experience the celebrations of life. They knew, after all, this was all too fleeting.

After all the gifts had been unwrapped and meals had been shared, their sweet little boy left this earth, leaving many with broken hearts. Grief shook foundations to the core. They were only able to fiercely love this little boy for just over a half of a year. According to my calculations, that is a whole lifetime minus seven months too short.

Although I was now living in a different state with distance standing in between, I reached out to offer my sympathy and support along with a large collection of others doing the same. There was nothing to give but prayer, kind words, and care. I told my friend I was well acquainted with ache, I understood pain, and I would be a listening ear if she was in need. I sent prayers and told her I would be a keeper of her complex feelings if she needed a safe place to go. I conveyed how I would help keep the memory of her son vivid, fresh, and new.

Much to my surprise and dismay, my friend lashed out in a hurtful response to my sympathy. Although I realized she was simply answering from under the shroud of pain, she said, "There is no way you could understand what I'm going through. You lost your babies before you met them. It's completely different for me, so don't tell me you understand the way I feel. It's worse than you could imagine. You don't know what it's like to have your child be a part of your life and then taken away. I know of other people who better understand, so I would much rather go to them instead of you."

As conversation continued, her words grew even more pungent. She said things I would rather not linger upon or repeat, but here's the point: by categorizing loss (and the complex feelings that accompany), she began to isolate herself not only from me, but from others she believed could never understand. She thought her wounds were bigger than mine, so I was not trusted with her pain. While I was incredibly hurt by her sharp words, I understood she was operating out of a place of defense. She did not wish to be misunderstood and didn't want the risk of possible further pain. She was building walls of protection while placing her pain on a hierarchy.

It is said that hurt people hurt people, but pain only turns you into a jerk if you allow it. It does not give you license to turn words into daggers or start fires with your tongue. We will all feel the ravages of death and difficulty in our lives. We will all face loss, and it is ALL pretty terrible. Pain is not to be used as an excuse to inflict more pain, for it's very good at multiplying on its own and doesn't deserve our help.

However, as it turns out, my friend's harsh words were not wasted because they taught me something important: we are NEVER in a position to categorize someone else's pain. While loss tells us we are alone on an island with our experiences, there is no way to rank our ache against that of another. Loss, after all, cannot be measured on any sort of Richter scale because its reach inside a human soul is incalculable. My pain does not hurt more than yours, and your gash is not deeper than mine. There is no way to feel all the complicated things hidden inside someone else's experience and say, "You cannot possibly understand, for my loss was worse than yours." That is not our privilege, nor is it our place. Even if we hurt so badly we believe it is capable of blatantly killing us, and even if we build protective walls around our hearts to prevent more hurt from getting through, we still have the ability to open our eyes and see that we all, at one point or another, feel this same way. Each one of us will be inflicted by some variation of soul pain so entirely wild, there is no possible way to define nor contain it within graded rankings.

We damage ourselves and others when we self-protect through angry words and self-centered comparisons. Joy and hope cannot possibly sprout from such soil. There are plenty of opportunities in this life that will inflict undesirable pain. In fact, until we die, they are a certainty. I have come to realize it is a beautiful thing when we cease isolating, stop comparing, and simply sit with each other through the pain without trying to categorize or even understand it.

Like a cluster of pierced moonflower seeds pressed into the soil next to each other, this is where we can help each other once again grow. Not through leaving anyone behind, overcrowding with our advice and opinions, categorizing and comparing, nor by staying soaked in our own pain, but through sitting next to each other in the new soil of camaraderie, we can help each other grow through our various aches. In allowing our hearts to break together, we can generously surround our shared pain with support. When we see, hold, and honor one another's grief, we allow ourselves to know and be known. Unspooling our complicated layers in front of each other without comparison shows us grief is a piece, even a requirement, of love. What a holy privilege. Truly, we are in this together. Loss is loss is loss.

those harsh words
leaking from the lips
of people who do not
understand
are seeds
to be buried
in soft soil
and sung to
sweetly and kindly
until a garden
of grace
grows lush
and towering
in their place

yes
a single seed
has ability
to produce a towering
vibrant bloom
but how much
more breathtaking
is an entire field
of flowers stretching
endless arms
across horizon
together
as one

Chapter 9

Frostbitten

A few years ago, we moved from the suburbs out into the country along with some of our family members. We desired a shared experience of spreading out, watching the glittering stars, listening to the quiet, and slowing our pace. And while I have never gardened much in my life outside of pulling weeds as a child in my parent's garden, there was now ample space to cultivate our own food. I envisioned heaps of ruby red soft tomatoes, crisp cucumbers, and piles of green beans but had little knowledge as to how to make it happen. Where I lack this knowledge, however, other family members of mine have tried-and-true experience.

In early spring of our first year in the country, we worked together to till old soil to prepare for our first garden. It had been several years since our newly acquired ground had been plowed, so well-established weeds had to be uprooted to make room for new health. Neglected soil required care and attention in order to produce our desired bounty.

As early spring rain sprinkled down on us, we turned the soil, pulled up weeds, fertilized, laid out stakes, marked rows, and pressed tiny little seeds into the ground of our large garden. We were so hopeful for the first year of gardening at our new home and watched daily as delicate green shoots began peeking up from the soil. It was exciting to see hard work begin to show itself in such a tangible way.

A couple weeks later, we awakened to frost clinging like crystals upon every outdoor surface. None of us realized temperatures would dip so unseasonably low and we certainly had not expected frost would fall. We were entirely unprepared. Our little plants had remained uncovered and susceptible throughout the night, and though the rising sun made every blade of grass shimmer with beautiful frosty morning gold, we knew our garden was in jeopardy. The little seeds we had excitedly planted into the ground may not have been strong enough to survive such a chill.

Much to our disappointment, a section of our garden did not survive. Some of those early seedlings that had begun to stretch tender arms out of the dirt were coated in frozen dew too heavy to carry. They were simply too delicate for the chill and not designed to survive such temperatures.

In all actuality, however, it was our fault the little veggies perished. We were not attentive enough to help protect against the surprise frost. Had we been more alert, we could have provided a covering for our plants to give them a better chance of weathering the harsh night.

We certainly learned a lesson in garden attentiveness through this experience, but I think a greater measure of wisdom can be pulled from our little cultivation tragedy. Just like seeds, we can survive the necessary processes to become ready for the soil. We can make it through the breaking, submersing, and planting. We can even begin to nuzzle down and stretch our roots into the richness of God's foundation; but once we begin to grow, how can we weather the various conditions that come our way? The answer is that we can both root ourselves in Christ and have Him as our covering—a nourishment from below based upon His foundational Word and protection from above.

While the vegetables we planted in our garden did not get the luxury of crying out to us in the middle of the night for covering in the cold, we do have the capability to call out to our very attentive God. Even though we may firmly plant ourselves in Him, there will constantly be elements at work against our growth. Flood rains may come, violent winds might blow, hungry critters or sneaky bugs may come for a visit, and frost might fall. Of course, these represent the various difficulties that will continue to present themselves in our own lives, whether in the form of losses, discouragement, stress, division, virulent sin, or various trying circumstances. Whatever they may be, they will come. However, we do not have to weather the elements without a covering. While a blanket would not have prevented frost from falling upon our garden, it would have protected our plants from becoming destroyed by the conditions. Likewise, having God as our covering will not prevent difficult circumstances from occurring, but it keeps us from succumbing to that which comes to steal, kill, and destroy.

How does one acquire this covering? From the knowledge of God's Word and worshiping Him as our first go-to action, yes, but also through constant communion with Him. A relationship. The kind of relationship a child has with a parent. Envision a small child waking in the middle of the night, trembling with fear from a terrible nightmare and plagued with a stomachache. When the child has a healthy relationship with their parent, there is no hesitation to cry out for help in the dark of night. At their call, the loving parent responds with haste. They come running to wrap comfort around what is difficult and terrifying. While the nightmare happened and the stomachache persists, a loving parent is simply present. Their nearness is what nurtures, consoles, and sees the child through the scariest of nights. While a loving parent is a covering far more comforting than an actual blanket, how much more caring is our God who is exceedingly able to provide all that is needed for weathering everything we face!

The presence of the Father makes all the difference. His nearness realized is our covering. Psalm 91:4 (NIV) says, *"He will cover you with his feathers, and under his wings you will find refuge; his faithfulness will be your shield and rampart."* When the elements continue to work against a newly flourishing seedling, He is the nourishment below and the covering above. In this soil, with this blanketing, our roots begin to stretch deep and vines begin to reach high no matter the surrounding elements. He is our safe place.

stay right here
and patiently wait
for the flowers
are about to bloom
and the sky will spill
the most delicious moonlight

Chapter 10

The Patient Gardener

Admittedly, I am not the greatest at keeping plants of any kind alive and thriving. This I have learned especially since moving out into the country. While several in my family seem to have been born with green thumb talent, I strive to keep flowers, plants, and vegetables healthy. Despite my efforts, I often fail, but I refuse to let that keep me from trying. Occasionally, I do manage to find a surprising measure of horticultural success, but never without a great amount of attentiveness.

A couple springs following our frost-coated blunder, Addie and I decided to plant moonflower seeds for the first time. After researching and waiting patiently for the right time, we nicked open the tough little moonflower seeds, soaked them in water, and began readying the soil in a large planter. We prepared the top eight inches of soil by tilling and lightly fertilizing, careful to add just the right amount—not too much, or the plant would produce vines void of blossoms. Addie and I pressed the split-open seeds into the soil, making certain not to overcrowd so there would be ample space for them to stretch out and grow. Then, keeping the dirt lightly watered, we waited patiently.

With time, and much to our delight, tender moonflower chutes slowly began to poke through the crust of brown earth. Chutes then transformed into thin, delicate vines that wrapped around the trellis support we had provided. Twisting and turning round and round, they climbed up the thin iron bars while reaching toward the sky. Success! While not every seed resulted in a growth, others pleasantly began to thrive. As we continued tending to the bed of soil, Addie and I watched the moonflower vines come alive.

Given the amount of attentive care required of us for these gardening adventures, viewing God as the Great Gardener of Souls causes me to think this is not an easy title to hold. My little moonflower seeds did not hold complex opinions or emotions. There were no cries or complaints as we cracked them open to soak and prepare them for the soil. They had no say in where they would be planted, or even if they would survive at all. It was up to us, the gardeners, to do the work.

When we identify with this metaphor of the moonflower seed, we realize we are like "seeds" ourselves who hold infinite complexities inside us. We are ridiculously more difficult than literal seeds because we are loud about our personal thoughts and our emotions easily steer the helm of our lives. As God cracks us open, soaks, plants, and tends to our lives, we have large opinions regarding how the process should both look and feel differently than He sees fit. He knows the right soil for our type of seed and has the exact measurements of water and fertilizer figured out. He knows how to arrange all the elements perfectly in order to create an environment fit for us to truly come alive. But oftentimes, the whole process is too uncomfortable and we choke out our own ability for future growth by allowing bitterness and opinion to root in place of intended health. Just as some of our own moonflower seeds did not survive, maybe this is where some of us remain for the rest of our lives—seeds stalled out in fertile soil. We are given everything we need to thrive but frequently do not accept it because it doesn't feel good.

God, our Great Gardener, is knowledgeable and trustworthy. He is an expert at growing the most luxurious, extravagant gardens and puts every expert to shame with His attentive skill. However, while in the process of "seeding," we often think we know what is best instead. If it's uncomfortable, we assume "this process means He is not good." If it is ugly, we have trouble envisioning how beauty could ever grow. If it hurts, we assume He does not know what's best, has forgotten us, or doesn't even exist. It seems easier at times to cross our arms, point our fingers, call God incompetent, and stay in a place of stunted growth.

But God is so patient, isn't He? He keeps giving us opportunity after opportunity to be tended by His loving hands no matter how much time we have wasted sitting in our bitter pain or strong opinions. Unlike actual seeds that have no say in their thriving or survival, we have a choice to accept His nurturing. We have the ability to shift our eyes past the initial infliction, through the residual anger and bitterness, and around to what is waiting on the other side. God may plant us, but unlike actual flowers, it is our choice if we will bloom as He intended.

It must be said, even when we do begin to thrive, we might push past the soil and find the sky void of expected sunny, cheery light. It might instead be a thick, black night. Life oftentimes looks quite differently than we anticipated, but that does not mean there's been a terrible mistake. It does not mean our existence won't be as rich and beautiful as we had hoped. Instead, it means we have been invited to bloom in unexpected ways that could quite thoroughly surprise.

what impatient people we are
so easy bowing to hurry
expecting every process be expertly expedited
every lesson instantaneously easy
without willingness
to invest
in the slow process
of growing towering blooms
from ordinary seed

a garden does not appear in one day
(or even in a few)
but over time
under tender
patient care

Chapter 11

Spring Always Comes

Those of us who live in the Upper Midwest are well acquainted with the disappointment found in a delayed unfolding of spring. After the hush of a long, frigid winter, we wait with anticipation for the opportunity to leave our long parkas at home and drench ourselves in the warmth of a late evening sunset. Following months and months of white and muted beige, our eyes crave the crisp colors found when cold loosens its grip. Spring is so very exciting because it feels like the entire world is releasing a held breath. It feels like a fantastic rebirth, a fresh chance.

When the process of spring seems to be stuck on pause, our mouths are stuffed full of complaints and our hearts brim with impatience. We find it very difficult to feel thankful while still shoveling snow in late April, so we grumble to each other and make (largely empty) threats to move someplace milder and greener. The snowflakes that brought wonder and magic in December tend to make our hearts bitter mere months later. Oh, how easily we tire of our surroundings and how quick we are to complain. Some of us even fall into depression because the wait can feel so very long. We desire to rush the transition from winter to spring because we want to feel more comfortable as quickly as possible. We want color, warmth, and long hours of honey-colored summer sunlight.

Isn't this much like our seasons of ache and loss? They feel so very drawn out, as though the chill will never release from our bones. Waiting for happier seasons seems like a slow, desolate process, as though the second hand of the clock has decided to measure hours instead. The surrounding terrain appears brown, barren, quiet, and lonely. Many of us mirror the darkness of winter, sinking into the ash of depression. The days are gray and cloudy and we wrap ourselves in impatience and self-pity. Are we stuck here forever? Is there anything good here in the seemingly endless wait? Will winter ever retreat?

Here is the truth: spring always comes, even if it is delayed. Here in the Upper Midwest, no matter how long it takes for winter to thaw, it does not stay forever. The trees will bud and bloom, the heat of mid-summer will arrive, and the seasons will continue to march on. In our own lives, the uncomfortable seasons can also pass. While this does not mean we won't hold memory and feeling of the hurt, and while it does not mean difficult seasons won't come again, it does ultimately mean such things are temporary. Circumstances are ever shifting. Nothing on earth stays still and unmoving. No season can remain forever.

Instead of viewing the long wait for spring as abandonment, what if it is a season of adoption? It is here we can realize we are no longer sons and daughters of temporary circumstance. Though we easily attempt to claim ownership over people, situations, and even time itself (and also believe such things hold shares of ownership over us), we can realize shifting seasons are not a place of eternal allegiance. What if in the wait we hear God say, "It is here My fidelity to you is a beacon of hope; for while everything around you is constantly shifting, I will always remain the same. You are Mine alone, and I have not abandoned. My arms are wide open and reaching for you. In My hands alone is found the healing of spring. Look past the chilled fog, and there I am. I will lead you to a new place in due time. You belong to Me, not your circumstances."

Even though it hurts, and even though we long to rush the season of wait, what if all the things that truly matter simply take time? Just as rushing a moonflower seed through the breaking process does not yield a richer bloom, and just as hurrying the arrival of spring will not make it sweeter, wishing away painful situations does not make us heal faster. There must be an "in between" time of wait. Refinement cannot be rushed.

Let us not allow our pain and impatience dictate our ability to see what is veracious: circumstances are ever shifting but God is not. There is not one moment of time when things do not change. Even if not perceived by the clouded eye, every person, place, and circumstance is in a continual state of transformation. The only thing certain in this life is change, and we do not have to remain slaves to one particular season of life. We do not have to stay as a split-open seed. We are not carelessly planted without our knowledgeable Great Gardener of Souls tenderly caring for us. Not for a moment does He cease to keep watch.

As for me, in between the point of our losses and the reality of "more" felt like an endless wait. At times, I still feel as though I am there, but this time is never wasted and it is never as stagnant as it seems. It is where I allow myself to become adopted and cared for by the One who knows me better than I know myself. It is where I learn I am not a daughter of disappointment and grief. My story will not end with loss, and it is not defined by what I do not have. Though our five babies are forever a part of my soul, the loss of their lives does not have to sour my hope. For where my hands are lacking, His fingers are laced between. In the waiting, He is constantly filling me with His presence. He is the MORE I desire. He is the spring—lush, abundant, and filled with hope.

And spring always comes.

Oh Lord—Master Designer of my soul—only You could look upon my cardboard castles and papier-mâché palaces and deem me worthy enough to inhabit as Your home.

For as soon as You pass through the windows finally flung open, my structures are reimagined and entirely refashioned. Mud is traded for gold, clay exchanged for rare jewels, sticks replaced with strength.

You transform dingy basement spaces into magnificent ballrooms and convert hidden attic places into regal banquet halls. You illuminate forgotten corners and repair rot lurking deep inside bones.

Because of You, my wastelands give way to mansions too rich to be appraised. Architect and artist, You replace poverty with the wealth of Holy Ground.

I set out on a voyage
to discover all that is beautiful
in the world
and safety
as I had known it
was not to be found

quests, after all
are built of mystery
and soon I found myself
eye-to-eye with grief
toe-to-toe with pain
captured in sorrow's embrace

there I felt
beauty interlaced
within dark strands
of midnight

for "safe" does not mean "here"
as though life has been
placed upon antiseptic shelves
likewise "beautiful"
is not to be held still

but experienced
in the full

I found beauty
not as a thing to be kept
but as a song
floating among
all that is wild

if today is numb
and you cannot feel
place your hand upon your chest
when all is quiet and still
and sense the metronome
throbbing deep inside your core
as the heart steadily whispers,
"I am here, I am here,
and there is so much more."

Chapter 12

Pressed Down

In time, the little moonflower seeds are scooped out of the water by a strong hand and gently pressed into soil. The seeds thought their piercing and drowning was the end, but now, sitting in the darkness of earth, they wait their first chance at life. Some go on to beautifully bloom, while others never become anything more.

If you recall, when Addie and I planted our moonflower seeds, some never grew. While several began to press upward, others remained dormant underground. Likewise, in our own broken-seeded state, we can easily choose to cease further growth. We can sit in the dirt with bitterness endlessly seeping through our open gashes like a bleeding that refuses to coagulate. While this would be an easier choice void of sacrificial movement forward, it is here gardens turn into graveyards. It is here growth can stunt as we remain stuck in our pain.

On the contrary, we have opportunity to experience what it is like for tiny roots to begin sprouting out of our wounds. Instead of forever bleeding out poison, our tears could serve as nourishment for new roots. Even prior to seeing what is above the ceiling of soil, we could begin to grow. Thin footings could begin to reach down into prepared ground.

While sitting in my own plot of darkened soil, I realized there must be more. I had survived what felt as though it should kill. God's presence had not only sustained me among all the breaking and remained through my questioning, but He was there in the dirt with me, too. The crevices of His fingerprints were caked with soil as He pressed me into my prepared place of planting. He felt textures of earth while tucking the soil overtop. He gently tended to me before I could see anything more. While I knew the breaking process well now, I was curious what would happen if I relaxed into waiting for what was to come.

Without truly knowing if I would ever fully flourish, I allowed small roots to begin growing from my wounds—an action I could never begin on my own accord. I could feel His presence in the imperfect. I knew He would never leave because He is the God who is in the dirt with me. Just as Moses told Joshua in Deuteronomy 31:8 (NIV), *"The Lord himself goes before you and will be with you; he will never leave you nor forsake you. Do not be afraid; do not be discouraged,"* I knew He was also with me. In response to this knowledge, and despite holding the aftertaste of grief in my core, I began to explore the surrounding fertile soil and wonder what was above. The Great Gardener of Souls was with me, and perhaps it was time to trust that He truly is who He says He is.

As I waited upon God's continual teaching and tending, I realized this: even in the painful breaking, even in the confusing drowning, even in the darkened dirt, I could breathe.

Part Two
Bloom

it is easy to unfurl
under a warm sunlit sky
but oh, my dear
you can do the same
even in the night

Chapter 13

Soft and Slow

"*Click, click, click,*" my shutter snapped, and I took a shallow breath while repositioning myself on the ground. I was photographing a plump, fuzzy bumblebee bouncing from bloom to bloom in our flower bed. In a display equally fascinating as adorable, the bee looked as though it had pulled a tiny black and yellow sweater over its belly before coming to feast on sweet nectar. I sat in the dirt wearing my wide-brimmed sun hat with my trusty old camera in hand, and the midday light warmed my shoulders. It was late June, and I found myself thankful for a lazy day to simply sit and enjoy a humming bee and vibrant blooms. Life had been so fast, as it often is, and I marveled at how it seemed like just yesterday I was stopping to smell the early spring lilacs lining the side of our country road. "How is it June already? I need to take more time to notice," I thought to myself. "I'm not sure I even realized when summertime arrived."

At what point does spring turn into summer? I know there is a date on the calendar, moon cycles, and a summer solstice to define what actual day summer arrives; but the subtle changes found in this transformation seem to slip by without too many people paying close attention. For instance, have you noticed which day delicate, new leaves take on a deeper, more mature hue? Have you realized which hour a crab apple tree begins to disrobe its blush petals? Do you keep track of which evening the fireflies begin to light their magical lanterns and dance like little jewels across the horizon? While we notice these wonders from time to time, they often unassumingly take place without our attention or admiration.

I set down my camera and placed my palms in the warmed soil in front of me. I felt like I was in a position of remembering. When did my "seed" turn into something more? My mind thumbed through the details that occurred to bring me past the shore of mere acceptance of my pain and into a place of feeling fully alive. I thought through the processes that ushered me into a life richer than I ever imagined despite very present difficulty. While change has the capability to be remarkably quick and swiftly grandiose, it is more often soft, subtle, and slow. Healing can be accelerated, but it often asks for plentiful time as personalized details are stitched anew. I have been soaked in ache, but I am now a towering bloom. This change certainly did not happen in one night. I have felt my way along the raw edges of grief and even sat inside its bountiful belly for years on end. I still felt the details of sorrow as I sat in the June sun photographing the beautiful day surrounding me, and I certainly will continue to do so in the future, but I am still here. I am whole. And everything looks quite differently than I envisioned.

When my broken-seeded existence finally began to grow past the dirt I was buried in, it was not a perfect, bright, sunny day I found waiting for me on the other side. Instead, it appeared to be more like that deep blue night sky—mysterious, full of hushed wonder and hard-earned night-vision sensibility. Life was different now. Loss had altered me. The moonflower has caught my attention so intently because it blooms here in this dark, unexpected environment. After all this time, I feel as though I can identify. I am doing the same. But how did I get here? I do believe if I point a magnifying glass at one concept, I can better map out the veins that have carried me to this star-laden landscape: *gratitude*.

I understand eye rolls may have just happened as you read that word. In the midst of pain, it is hard to ingest the flavors of gratitude, isn't it? "There's nothing here that is good, so let me just sit with my pain and not be okay for a while," you might say. Yes, it is necessary (and often important) to feel the layers of pain instead of running from it or dulling it through temporary means; however, can *staying* in this spot bring lasting health? Has insisting upon making a permanent home inside distress brought about peace? Has worry ever accomplished anything? Has anxiety ever been a good friend? The answer to these questions is a resounding "NO."

It is God IN these feelings WITH me that makes the difference. He sits with me in the dirt of my pain, and it is only through His near presence that hidden goodness is revealed as a lush, blooming garden. He is the One who brings about the transformation. He is the One who takes my hand and gives me strength to move again. He is the only One who induces gratitude as He opens my eyes to see how imperfection can set the stage for beauty. He allows me to see there is much to be thankful for even when I do not initially perceive it. When gratitude feels impossible, He alone can teach me how to find it within the tiniest of crumbs. And once found in small, sweet measures, my appetite quickly hungers for more. Gratitude then turns from following a thin line of honey to discovering the whole entire pot.

Thankfulness turns tears into nourishing waters capable of transforming desert places into holy ground. It bids me to slow down and opens my pupils to see the details of this grand life even in dim light. It causes me to empty myself in order to be filled anew. It allows me to see what is hidden. It brings joy beyond what is found within the layers of my own will. It coexists with ache and enhances the truths of God's Word. And while gratitude never comes with a promise of changing my situations into what I would deem ideal, it serves as a teacher, encouraging me to thrive despite.

Bloom.

If you are still alive and breathing, it is not too late for you to find this place for yourself. But it might not be what you have expected. Exhale. While your arms might be overflowing with ache, there is always room for hope and gratitude. There is always space to entertain the idea that it is fully possible to enjoy life as it is right here, right now, no matter the surrounding situations and no matter the pain.

There in the dirt of my flowerbed, I smiled as the bumblebee rested on a petal. *Click.* I snapped another photograph to catch the wonder of the small moment. And this is why I am writing now. It has all mattered, and it is all worth remembering. The good, the bad, and all the mundane melt together to make a story worth telling. It all contributes and testifies to how it is possible to transform from a broken-open "seed" to an unexpected "bloom."

today
I stood underneath
an umbrella of blooms
and listened to the
humming chatter
of a thousand bumblebees
fluttering in the blue

isn't it something
how they sing in the light
but spin nectar to honey
in places hidden dark as night

perhaps the sweetest of things
happen when the rest of the world
is looking the other way

maybe your arms
are tired and trembling
because you have been
wearing the weight
of an entire universe
instead of simply living

Chapter 14

Tears

Have you ever met someone who wears kindness so generously it makes them entirely magnetic? My dear friend Kayla is one of those brilliant people who attracts others into her orbit simply through the way she lavishes love. When you are with her, she makes you feel as if you are one of the most important people in her world. On a muggy afternoon, as I was sitting across from her sharing lighthearted conversation at a mutual friend's graduation party, I witnessed her sweet kindness effortlessly at work.

Kayla's little children were buzzing around our table in the usual way kids do—fighting, giggling, and everything in between. Suddenly, one of Kayla's daughters came from around the house with the saddest frown painted on her face. Kayla drew her up into her arms and asked, "Oh my sweet one, what's the matter?" With chin quivering and voice wavering in an attempt to hold back a torrent of tears, her daughter explained she had fallen and hurt herself behind the house on the water slide that had been set up for all the visiting kids.

"That must have really hurt," responded Kayla. Then,

looking her little one straight in the eye, she quietly asked, "Do you need to cry?"

A nod of "yes," and Kayla's daughter dug her face into her mama's shoulder. There, in safe arms holding her tightly, she allowed soft sobs and crocodile tears to break free. After a few moments of release, she hopped up, wiped away tears, and headed back out to play.

The party went on and conversation fell back into rhythm, but I kept replaying this scenario in my mind. While it was a fleeting, everyday moment, I paused and pressed it into memory. The following day, I texted Kayla and told her how remarkable I found her interaction with her daughter. Kayla went on to explain this particular child of hers is usually very private and reserved with her emotions. She could tell her daughter needed to release tears but didn't feel as if she had permission to fully feel the sadness of her temporary injury. "So I asked her if she needed to cry because I could tell she needed to. We do this with all our kids, because we want to make sure they know we are a safe space for them to feel all the emotions they might be too afraid to explore," Kayla explained.

Her daughter knew that in her mother's safe, gentle arms, she could feel what she needed to. She did not have to "suck it up"; she could feel the pain, however momentary it was, and then carry on. This was where she found safety. What a beautiful thing to witness, and it definitely jogged my thoughts. I have spent so much of my life not permitting myself to truly *feel*. I have bottled up, ignored, and apologized for simply shedding tears. Why? What has limited me? Why do I feel the need to apologize for crying, and how has this possibly complicated my ability to heal? It has likely been fear.

I understand emotions should not be crowned the rulers of my life, as they are fickle, feral things. However, just as Kayla's daughter needed a moment to cry before going back to playing with her friends and siblings, I need to permit myself moments to cry, feel, and release. While emotions should not rule, they deserve to be explored, even if it means facing the fear of feeling, expressing, and practicing vulnerability.

It is okay to sit and feel pain even while moving forward. Experiencing the long-reaching waves of lingering sadness does not mean we are broken; it means we're human. And speaking of waves, have you ever noticed they do not end? Yes, they roll, swell, dance, and crash, but they are always alive and changing. Waves build into towers only to sink low. They lap on the shore only to magnetically retreat and form another. Waves don't die; they transform. And when they crash to the surface and reach to the sky, they are transparent. So it is with emotions. We each hold an ocean-full of feeling inside of our core, ever shifting, ever changing. They don't die; they change. There are times of calm, times of turmoil, and moments found in the in-between. All of these feelings exist not to rule but to be noticed. They are there to be FELT. And when they rise enough to bring transparency, they are in their most remarkable state.

So I ask you, do you need to cry? There is a safe space for us to do this. Yes, while we may have people in our lives who hold us, listen, and understand, the strong, capable arms that uphold the entire universe are also open to us. God, in all His majesty, cares enough to come close and hold us as we feel all the complexities of this life. He is the One who created us to feel emotion, as life without feeling would be incredibly robotic. Therefore, we do not have to clean ourselves up before we approach Him. We can run to Him—the very Jesus who wept—and bury our heads in His chest, crying all the tears we need to. God is a safe space to transparently feel the complexities of emotion and release what is needed. He is quite alright if we question, pound our fists, utter angry words, and cry an ocean of tears and snot onto His shoulder.

While reading through the Gospels, we see Jesus felt the

same things leading up to His crucifixion. In Luke 22:44, we learn He was so deeply distressed, His sweat turned into blood. We read about how Jesus petitioned and questioned His crucifixion (Matthew 26:39; Matthew 27:46), and we are told He wept over the death of His friend Lazarus (John 11:35). We do not approach a God who is too lofty and distant to understand our feelings. He has felt pain, ache, loss, and sadness, just as we do.

In Psalm 56:8 (NLT), King David says to God, *"You keep track of all my sorrows. You have collected all my tears in your bottle. You have recorded each one in your book."* God's arms are a place where our tears do not simply fall and disappear. They hold meaning. They are stored, remembered, and recorded. In His arms, we are free to bravely cry and feel because He deeply cares and understands. He is not a God who is aloof and far off, for He has worn flesh and bone and fully knows. I am incredibly thankful we serve a God who is so personable. "What a friend we have in Jesus," the old song goes. He is not just our friend in the daylight, He is ever so close in the saddest of nights. He is the only one who can calm raging seas inside of us with just one word from His mouth and touch from His hand.

I ask again, do you need to cry? You have permission. If you have been told to "suck it up and be a man," remind yourself that Jesus, the greatest man to have ever walked the planet, allowed Himself to weep. Perhaps actually permitting ourselves to feel is among the bravest of things we can do. Let your tears fall on His safe shoulders, but also, let them fall to the ground to water the soil for what is to come. This is where our season of blooming can begin—not by refusing to feel, but by permitting ourselves to explore our emotions, crying without coating our tears in apology, and feeling that which demands to be felt. Sorrow and lament do not stifle very well. They do not settle to the bottom of our souls only to disappear. They rise to the surface like waves and ask for our attention.

For the moonflower to grow, there must be moisture.

Whether rain, sprinkler, or watering can, the seeds must drink while planted in the dirt. Likewise, for us to live life as intended, we must not be afraid to wet our own cheeks with tears and let them stream down to the soil in which we are. These tears can nourish and renew. This process is more than simply permitting tears to fall; it is about allowing ourselves to feel. Destructive habits exist for so many because it seems easier to numb the pain than to actually feel, face, and release. Numbing only prolongs the ache. Feeling gives it space to be free. Allowing feelings to be felt not only sets them (and ourselves) free, but it also allows us to see it is quite a gift to be able to feel. And perhaps, this is worship, too.

Just as it is with any foliage, it is possible to overwater the moonflower. Likewise, there must come a time when our Great Gardener both tenderly collects our tears and then dries our eyes with His steady presence while gently leading us to His pastures of peace. Tears are nourishing for a time, but He alone holds the lasting comfort we crave.

oh, but if you do not
press deeply into
the sadness
wetting your hands
with its sticky pulp
how will you ever uncover
the hidden treasure
awaiting underneath

weeping is memory
come to life

sea glass
velvet sky
weathered and worn
silken edges
coated milky white
resting in the palm
lapping onto shores
woven among clouds
hidden in your eyes
delicate as a whisper
supple as a sigh
tumbled through waves
broken treasure made
softer, kinder, new
you are this particular
shade of light blue

Chapter 15

Amber Gems

On an early summer night, I watched in wonder as a storm unfurled over the countryside surrounding our home. With my husband and daughter already tucked into bed, I reclined alone next to our patio window to watch blades of lightning slice through ashen sky. Portly raindrops tapped heavily upon both roof and window, and wind caused tree branches abundant with new leaves to bow toward the ground. The sky's voice rumbled and groaned with unsettled energy. I observed the grumbly display until the storm clouds moved east on assignment to water other grounds. The night slowly turned quiet once again, and I tiptoed to bed.

As darkness gave way to a new day, morning sun peeked above the horizon and splashed golden light over the fields. I drew open the shades and noticed the night's raindrops still clinging to glass—evidence of a storm that had once been. While a few drops slipped down the window like leftover tears, the amber sun glistened globes of light inside each one. Morning luminance enveloped inside yesterday's rain; what a simple, commonplace delight all too easily overlooked.

Tucked inside this scene of water and light set upon glass is

Amber Gems

a truth: yesterday's storms existed and were very real. Those unsettled rain clouds did indeed roll through. Their effects are tangible and lasting, but the storms themselves came to an end. In the teardrops of yesterday's tempest, the sun of a fresh day intermingles. Water and light—a nourishing combination.

Pain and hope do not have to be separate entities. In fact, they are fully capable of existing together. Pain can set the stage for hope's brilliant illumination. Just as a little burst of new-day sunshine sits like a bit of warm honey inside of a raindrop, there is a brilliant measure of God's light found like treasure amongst our leftover stormwaters.

Little amber gems glowing within the boundaries of water droplets—what a gorgeous scene. Before I went about with the rest of my day, I entertained this thought: within the glass walls of lasting ache shines diamonds of hope. We must be willing to constantly look through the remnants of the storms in order to see them. The best gems are usually not found out in the wide open. Like searching for treasure, we must be willing to break away from the blinding mundane to find the gems tucked inside that which appears to be void of goodness.

how can it be
the same sun rises
in obedience every day
yet its light is
new and different
in every possible way

Chapter 16

The Power of a Name

When we moved to Wisconsin for a new youth pastoral position nearly a decade ago, one of the first people we met was Beth. In fact, she called us even prior to our cross-state move simply because she wanted to introduce herself and make us feel welcome in our new church and youth group. Beth had been a youth leader for quite some time, and I quickly learned she had so much patience and gentleness when it came to relating to the teenage girls in our new church. She always possessed a knack for making the girls feel seen and heard, frequently meeting for coffee or inviting them into her home for discussions that were too long for normal Sunday mornings at church. She held Bible studies, shuttled teenagers around for youth events, came on mission trips with us, and selflessly served above and beyond expectation.

More than a ministry partner, she quickly became a dear friend. She and I are both avid readers, so we swapped books and discussed plot lines for hours on end. We spent a fair amount of afternoons sipping tea and lemonade, talking about anything and everything through laughter and tears. I always loved her enthusiasm to discuss what she had been reading in the Bible and admired her eagerness to ask questions as she explored God's Word and character at greater depth. Her eyes were open wide to the ways God wanted to work in her life, and she held a growing desire to see others fall in love with Jesus, too.

When my mom had a stroke a few years ago, she put together a basket of items to bring cheer during recovery. Of course, Beth made sure to include devotional books and Scripture to keep my mom encouraged as she began her healing process. Pointing others to Jesus in their times of need had always been Beth's specialty. She lavished great love upon the teenagers, my family, and me.

A few years ago, Beth and her husband sat on our living room couch and, with tears rolling down their cheeks, told us she was entering her second battle with cancer. Beth had been cancer-free for many years, but it had now returned in a vicious and possibly terminal form. They did not know what was ahead, but they were saddened. They knew the difficult ins and outs of wrestling with cancer, and they were about to experience it all once again. This time it was Beth and her family in need of encouragement.

From the start of her second diagnosis, Beth held such confident peace despite all the sticky, sad feelings that inevitably came. She knew the same God who held provision in all her good days also embodied faithfulness and strength in times of sickness. In those days plagued with illness, she frequently came to church and spent time quietly praying and hashing her feelings out with God in our sanctuary. Quiet times with the Lord were opportunities she eagerly sought out, as simply being with God added to the ferocious strength welling up inside of her. When I joined her in prayer one afternoon, she looked at me and said, "No matter what, I will never stop worshiping God. There is so much to be thankful for, and through this sickness, He is showing how near to me He really is. The lessons He has been teaching me have been so rich. He's not leaving me, and I won't leave Him."

Fast forward a few months, and Beth found out she would have to endure chemotherapy nicknamed "Red Devil" after its crimson color and wicked side effects. She knew what laid ahead would not be fun for her body to endure, but she looked me square in the eyes and said, "Sarah, I'm renaming this thing. No Red Devil will be entering my body because I've decided to call it 'Rose.' I have to believe God has goodness hidden in this thing for me. So, 'Rose' is a name that will bring me so much more hope than the alternative."

Beth could not change her circumstance, but she did change her mindset to one of hope and gratitude. Because of this level-headed, God-given strength, she was able to peer past her sickness and perceive possible opportunities of blessing that only this particular situation could bring. In fact, she was about to meet people through this treatment (and the various treatments to follow) who would greatly enrich her life. In her months of chemotherapy, she told so many stories about people she was able to pray for and encourage. In turn, she met others who ministered deeply to her in her own times of need. Through her cancer treatments, she became aware. She kept serving. She made friends. Even on her toughest days, she kept thriving. Truly, even amidst her chemotherapy experience, she blossomed like a beautiful rose.

Renaming her struggle did not mean her life became exponentially easier. Beth still experienced side effects. She had extremely tough days. She grieved over her illness and felt so many waves of sadness. However, the mental shift of renaming her cancer drug gave Beth wider eyes to see the grander picture. It allowed space for Beth to declare her sickness and subsequent treatments would not have the power to dictate her mind, will, and emotions.

What a concept to chew on.

What a reality to adopt!

In the same way a red devil was transformed into a rose, what if we took on the regular habit of renaming our struggles in order to better see the masked beauty they have the potential to embody? This would, in essence, be a dismantling and disarming of the powers of darkness and negativity. It would be faith in action centered around the eternal goodness of God instead of the temporary gravitational pull of difficulty. Renaming struggles would give fresh opportunity to see God's hand at work. It would shift our worship to God instead of bowing to circumstance. It would mean feeling pain but not elevating it onto a pedestal of authority.

Difficult circumstances are like needy toddlers. The demands they give are constantly shifting and shouting for attention. "Look at me!" they impose. "I need your concern!" It is incredibly easy to pour every ounce of energy upon them because that is what they seem to require. (And all the mothers of littles say a resounding "amen!") However, a challenging toddler does not usually generate the strength needed to care for itself. The wisdom, resources, and ability to care for their needs must come from an outside source.

Renaming our struggles would not be pretending they don't exist, nor would it be turning a deaf ear to their cries. Renaming would be a focal shift while allowing God to become the source of our strength. Renaming the worst of the worst could turn pain into opportunities of worship and tools of gratitude for even the most wearied hands.

Beth taught all of us so many things during her illness, and through her example, we saw what it looks like when someone takes control out of cancer's grip and places it into God's capable care. Through this, she showed us it is possible to rename the worst into worship; and because of this, not an ounce of red devil entered her body—only a red, blooming, liquid rose.

Renaming turned poison into beauty.

Renaming turned the worst into worship.

I will do the same.

To me, "loss" will now mean "deeper life while I am here."

"Miscarriage" will now mean "an opportunity to realize the sacred in a fuller sense."

"Ache" will now mean "God is truly near to the broken-hearted."

"Death" will now be called "TEMPORARY."

What, now, do YOU have the opportunity to rename?

after all
it mustn't be about surviving
merely making it through
but about collecting
armfuls of memories
until it feels as though
your heart could overflow
with every
wildly good
deeply painful
syrupy sweet
awfully dreadful
scary and thrilling
brief and fleeting
thing

this is what
life should be
after all

sorrow carves canyons
into boring layers
of safe souls
and fills hollow spaces
with the most remarkable gold
for if we lived
and never lost
how could we ever realize
the wild value
in it all

Chapter 17

Poison in the Bones

The silky-white petals of a moonflower look as though they were painted from the milk of moonlight. Angelic. Ethereal. Pure. As the blooms bathe in summer starlight, it is difficult to believe they come with a warning: poison lies hidden within their structures.

On the back of our moonflower seed packet, a brief alert was printed: *highly toxic if ingested.* I was curious to know more, so I did a bit of research. It seemed every website page dedicated to this flower included this same warning. "Do not allow humans or animals to eat any part of this flower." While simply touching moonflowers will do no harm, every part, from seed to blossom, contains harmful substances capable of greatly sickening anyone who ingests them. Symptoms range from hallucinations, increased blood pressure, confusion, and agitation, all the way to severe toxicity and death. In fact, many people who have attempted to get a "quick high" by allowing this poison into their bodies have been greatly harmed by its effects.[1]

While I was not at all interested in ingesting our moonflowers, I did find all of this to be quite interesting. Moonflowers not only uniquely bloom in the nighttime hours, but they do so while containing hidden poison. One would not know merely by looking at their leafy vines and robust flowers such toxicity is nestled inside their beauty, but it is indeed a part of their makeup. They know the taste of poison deep in their bones yet continue to bloom under the night sky.

I have tasted the poison of loss. It is a part of me. It has deeply changed me, but I am still here. Like the moonflower, I am living and "blooming" even with such poison etched into my DNA. If I had waited until all traces were undetectable to begin this process, perhaps I would have never given myself the opportunity to thrive once again on this side of heaven.

It is through tasting the poison of loss I have noticed the sweetness of life with increased intensity. This makes me wonder if I would have had the ability to detect all the layers of beauty in my life without my poison-laced experiences. Do we truly know what sweet is until we have tasted bitter, salty, or sour? In truth, we can define what sweet is because we have knowledge of contrasting tastes. Brought into the context of grief, I did not realize what I truly had in life until I was introduced to loss. Even though I have experienced such ache and have its lasting poison in my bones, my arms are filled with so much goodness. I have so very much. It took loss for me to fully perceive this truth.

After our miscarriages, I reached a realization. I was so entirely caught up in what I did not have, my attention failed to land on what I had right in front of me. I constantly wished for my ideals to come into fruition the way I planned in my own mind, so I had come to believe my full hands were empty instead. It was as though what I did have was invisible in the face of disappointment. My sight was focused on the horizon of what could be, not on the bountiful here and now. I was striving so hard to grow our family that my longings had consumed most of my time, effort, thought, and emotion.

While there was no particular "turning point" moment of clarity, such realization came slowly, like a gentle waking from slumber. With time, I no longer desired to be poked with needles, tested for medical issues, or given further rounds of new medication. I decided I wanted to enjoy life as it was, with what and who I had in front of me. I began to see how short and fragile life is. It can be snatched away in an instant, and I didn't want to waste any more time focusing on what was lacking. I wanted to learn how to drain every drop of sweetness available to me in the present. Once I started exploring, I quickly realized the beauty of life is a bottomless, bountiful well.

Please do not misread me in this; there is nothing wrong with bringing the desires of our hearts to the throne of God. There is absolutely no fault in asking Him to work on our behalf while presenting our needs to Him. However, when I began changing the narrative of my prayers from "God, please give me what I desire" to "God, help me to see the beauty in what You have given to me right now," my eyes began to open to the gorgeous bits found in this tragic and miraculous gift called life. Hear me: I did not give up on the miraculous, but I longed to look for all the ways it was already happening all around me. I longed to discover what I had been previously too blind to see. After tasting so much bitter, I was hungry for a larger measure of sweet.

I ceased striving for what I did not have and began a quest to realize the goodness already sitting in my open palms. I had come to believe only another successful pregnancy could correctly add abundance to our lives; and though the ache of losing sweet babies would forever reside inside my bones, I began to consider all the other ways my life was wonderfully full. Exploring gratitude began here: not denying myself grief nor giving up on the miraculous, but opening myself up to the idea that an incredible amount of goodness could be found in the places and situations I had not previously considered capable of such a yield. I had been waiting for the perfect scenarios to unfold in the most spectacular sunlight—the places where happiness and contentment make the most natural sense. However, joy is not always packaged in such obvious ways. Oftentimes, it is waiting to be discovered quietly in unassuming places.

Just as one cannot truly comprehend the taste of sweet without the presence of bitter, perhaps I would never realize the value of the temporary without experiencing loss. So yes, joy can co-exist with ache and gratitude can live entwined with pain. These things do not have to be separate in order to be fully realized. In fact, they are not fully defined without each other. Loss has illuminated the reality that everything before my eyes is constantly changing, passing, and remaking. If I spend my lifetime doing everything but noticing all the ways I can be grateful for my imperfect, brief hours and days, then I am wasting precious time. I am here for but a moment; so yes, I will grieve and I will ache, but I have decided to be attentive to all these passing details with a growing measure of gratefulness.

Stretching high and beautiful in the night sky, the moonflowers have poison coursing through their veins. It is part of their reality, their structure, and their DNA, yet they unfold in such a miraculous way. For my remaining moments on this earth, I will continually choose to do the same.

I want to live slowly
tasting every minute
holding every moment
upon my tongue
deciphering all the seasoning
hidden inside each one

were it not for the bitter
sweet would remain undefined
so I will bravely taste
and I will carefully savor
all of life's
intricate flavors

you cannot tell me
after watching the setting sun
spill lemon honey over meadows
and listening to coffee hum
while its percolating
or bending your mouth
into a smile that melts
the dew of evening
that today
or any day
is unremarkable
and ordinary

today
and every day
is miraculous
astonishing magic
and with each marigold sunrise
and in every violet sunset
we are given
the lavish gift
of right here
right now

Chapter 18

And She Heard the Birds

Recently, my dear friend Amy experienced the tragedy of having to say a very quick "goodbye" to a loved one. Her mother, a very foundational piece of her family, experienced a brief illness that wrung through her body. On a December afternoon surrounded tightly by Amy and the family who loved her so dearly, she surrendered to her illness and left this earth.

The months following brought a collection of feelings to the surface for my friend. This is how it is after loss. So many feelings pass through while you try to wrap your head around the fact that an important person has now been removed from the rest of your future here. Profound sadness, anger strong enough to shatter stone and build walls, love deep enough to dig wells, nostalgia so painful and sweet—all of it was felt by Amy.

In my conversations with Amy following her mother's passing, I noticed one particular feeling bubbling to the top with frequency: regret. She thought of all the times she may have hurt her mother's feelings with sharp words. She also imagined conversations that should have happened and softer phrases that could have been uttered. She thought of situations she could have handled differently and pieces of their relationship she might have changed. Amy's mind was easily filled with "should've, could've, would've" scenarios tinged with remorse.

Four months after her mother's passing, I was getting ready to enter our church sanctuary for Sunday morning service. Heading in the opposite direction, Amy breezed past me wiping red, puffy eyes. It was quite apparent my friend was having a rough morning, so I turned around to follow her. Taking Amy by the arm, I pulled her in for a hug and asked her if she was alright.

Through falling tears, she explained her mother had always loved birds. Spring and summer were filled with phone calls and texts about her various bird-watching observations. Her mom loved to describe the different birds she noticed throughout the months, but her very favorite thing to remark upon was the beauty of their morning springtime songs.

Amy, busied with raising her three children, did not easily see the value her mother held in bird-noticing. In fact, all the messages and remarks sent her way about birds annoyed her at times. "Mom, I don't care about birds like you do, and I really don't see what the big deal is," Amy would respond. Her mom didn't get the cue and persisted in sharing her bird-watching endeavors. In spring and summer, Amy could count on hearing one-way conversations as her mom continued to gush about her favorite feathered friends.

Now that the conversations had gone silent, Amy heard a bird singing early on that Sunday morning and felt the pang of regret. Oh, what she would give to hear her mom talk about the birds again, and she thought of all the ways her passiveness may have hurt her mom. Through tears, Amy said to me, "This morning I listened to the birds singing, and it was like I was hearing them for the very first time. I never noticed them quite like that before. I never cared. But there I was this morning, hearing the birds, and I felt so incredibly terrible about the way

I never cared when my mom was so excited about them. I asked God if there was any way He could redeem this. It's too late for me to go back and change the way I responded to my mom, but I feel so terrible."

After hearing the birds singing, she went along with her morning routine and headed to church. As service was beginning, she received a text from her father, a man who never once remarked about the wonder of birds. In his text, he told Amy he was listening to the birds singing outside of his home earlier that morning. How beautiful it was, and he wanted to tell Amy about it. After reading his text, she became completely overwhelmed and quickly exited the sanctuary.

"I can't talk to my mom about the birds anymore, but I can still talk to my dad. The fact he noticed the birds this morning just as I did is amazing. He never seemed to care before. And he texted me today of all days... the same day I am asking God to somehow redeem this," Amy said while wiping her eyes.

It was too late to change conversations with her mother, but she was now given an opportunity to respond to her father. While this wasn't exactly a "second chance," it was a "new chance." The loss of her mother was greatly tragic, but her eyes opened wider to what she had in this world. While noticing the birds singing in and of itself is a beautiful thing, greater truths were unlocked inside her heart—appreciation for the small yet significant wonders and God's amazing redemption.

Amy's mother is likely not spending her time in heaven counting all the times her daughter brushed her excitement to the side. Heaven does not include grudges in its halls, after all. Grievances and regret bring sorrow, and sorrow is not an eternal reality for those who call heaven their home. In fact, if birds are this fascinating here on earth, how much more enchanting will they be in heaven? Her mom could very well be enjoying the most otherworldly birds this very moment without a care as to what is happening here on earth. Regret is only felt by those of us who have not made it there yet. However, God's great redemption has the absolute power to silence regret and strip it of power.

I urged Amy to go home after church, set a chair up outside, and close her eyes to listen for the birds with open ears and a renewed heart. And she did just that. She's seeing the birds in a whole new light while noticing all their little fascinating details. The loss of her mother has been profoundly wounding, but Amy's eyes are now open wider not just to the birds, but to living in a greater appreciation for what is in the here and now. Regret cannot change her past, but redemption is altering her present.

And today, she hears the birds.

sorrow
flutters in
through windows
somehow left
wide open
and settles heavily
upon my chest
once again

I looked at its details
so familiar
so memorized
and said,
"I know you now
And I am no longer afraid.
Come and go
As you may."

this one, brief, delicious life
with its intricate veins
and delicate feathers
is bold and soft
awful and wondrous
sweet and overwhelming
and altogether delicate
here for a moment
swept away in the next
never quite certain
which breath will be the last
so I will sink deeply
into the fullest of flavors
unafraid of tasting
(and of feeling)
while juice slowly rolls
down my chin
for right now
the fruit is ripe
and for the taking
but this, I know
it is never
for my keeping

Chapter 19

Songs of Deliverance

I have heard it said walking is one of the best forms of physical exercise, but I am also thoroughly convinced it is one of the wisest practices for maintaining mental and spiritual health. Through the years, I have developed the routine of walking a few miles a day as often as my schedule allows. I walk outdoors in every season, including those less-than-ideal weather situations such as rain, snow, sub-zero temperatures, and blistering heat.

However, those gorgeous, early summer evenings when conditions grace our presence like an opening courtesy of a dance are my most favorite of walking conditions. You know... the kind of gentle, warm evenings that you wish could be captured inside a mason jar and cracked open amidst the chill of winter. However, no matter the weather—pleasant or otherwise—I walk because it has become a practice in which I hash, heal, learn, listen, notice, and feel.

My average walking pace is about three miles per hour, and it is quite astounding how many details one can observe while moving at that slow of a speed. At quicker paces, the details of a lush, silky vine creeping up a tree trunk are not fully noticed, the dewdrop nestled in a fuzzy leaf bed is passed over, and a bluebird hopping along as it hunts for lunch among softened ground goes ignored. Walking is the perfect opportunity to adore all the details hurry blinds us from. More importantly, at three miles an hour, I am given the perfect opportunity to hear the voice of God. A walk at this pace generously grants space for unhurried conversation—for talking, listening, noticing, responding, calming, and quieting. While I don't remember exactly when I gave my walks a name, I have come to refer to them simply (yet profoundly) as my "walks with Jesus." I imagine Jesus walking right by my side as though I were strolling along with one of my dearest of friends. Our feet rhythmically hit the pavement together as we indulge upon shared, unhurried time.

On a warm evening in early June, I went for a walk as the day was giving way to a glorious, tangerine-tinted sunset. In the near perfection of the moment, I became acutely aware of how significant it was to be walking with the One who orchestrated it all. The original artist who crafted such visual, tangible poetry surrounding all my senses was walking the pavement with *me*. This genius, the One from whom all other beauty and creativity flows, was keeping pace next to me as a friend. That thought in and of itself was incredibly profound and overwhelming. In response to the realization of His near presence that evening, my heart began to flutter as though a thousand butterflies scurried about in my chest. It was the first time I had felt such intimate nearness to our Creator.

In that moment, I began speaking to Him, telling of how humbling it was to share time with the One who imagined into existence the freshly blooming daisies dotting the roadside. Those flowers were His idea—an overflow of His imagination. I noticed their rounded centers of marigold that sat like little dollops of sunlight among the petals. "If there is such beauty here on earth," I wondered, "what would heaven bring about?"

I tipped my chin up to the sky, tear beads collecting in my eyes. I noticed how the clouds meandered by like moving sculptures against the blue. The greatest Creator of all time, the One who made all this by perfect design, was right beside me. Yes, how profound.

As I marveled, He softly began to speak to my listening ears. He told me He loved me, and said it made Him smile that I would take time to notice all the details He constantly creates. He told me I was His creation, and the same way I adore all the beauty around me, He adores the details lovingly assigned to me. I felt so seen as He gazed at me. I have knowledge God created me, but to feel deep inside my soul He is incredibly fond of all the parts of me was absolutely humbling. The same God who painted the sunset and scattered the clouds assigned every cell to my body and keeps track of every hair on my head. And He was not distant but near enough to feel His voice upon my soul.

As our conversation unfolded, I told Him how astounding it was to know that while He was fully present with me, He was doing the same for countless others across the globe at the very same time. He did not divide Himself, giving me a fraction and someone else a sliver. Instead, He is fully there for every single one of us with undivided attention. His omnipresence is something I have a hard time comprehending, to say the least. In response, He answered, "That's just who I am. Even though you do not understand all My ways, do you trust Me?" I answered, "How could I not?"

I imagined Jesus taking my hand much like we did in that vision He gave me so many years ago, and we walked together in beautiful silence for quite some time. There was not a romantic love shared between us, only this crazy, holy love that human language cannot quite pinpoint. So much deeper than friendship, more intimate than marriage, immeasurably further than family. That is His love for not only me, but you and every person on this earth. On that June evening walk, I felt this truth so fully. And even though I have failed so many times, God is always beside me, looking at me and loving me. Even though there is ache in this temporary life designed for expiration, He is present through every loss, joy, and complex feeling.

I then sensed something so profound—His presence wrapped around me as though I was garmented in a cloak. It felt like safety. It felt like joy. It felt like a beautiful, all-consuming song wrapping itself inside, outside, and all around my soul. At that moment, I realized nothing would come my way that He would not experience with me. I never understood this passage found in Psalm 32:7 (NIV) prior to this moment. *"You are my hiding place; you will protect me from trouble and surround me with songs of deliverance."* I had to feel this verse in action in order to grasp it. And when I felt His fatherly presence swirl all around me like a garment, like a sweet song—both at once—I realized His presence was the deliverance I had been seeking. His presence is like the sweetest song that does not end. His presence delivers me through the worst situations. I don't ever want to remove this covering from my life.

All of this was experienced on a simple summer walk. As daylight gave way to dusk, I truly felt as though I was blooming in His presence and under His attentive eye. While I don't always have such defining moments while walking, as long as I'm with Jesus, it is always profound. I could easily walk our country roads and neglect the fact He is next to me, waiting to listen and respond. I must constantly choose to use this time to daily commune with Him. No matter how I am feeling, this is where I can pause my soul to meet with Him. This is where I am reminded of who He is. This is where I am given the opportunity to sense the truth that He is my ever-present covering.

"Come near to God, and He will come near to you," James 4:8 (NIV) tells us. He does not force Himself upon us but gives us

the choice to pursue His love and the healing that gushes from it. God loves us too deeply to force this relationship, but when we choose to gaze at Him, He pulls us so very close. Through my practice of walking and discovering the truth of His nearness, I have come to learn the details of His character and recognize the softness of His voice. I have felt His fatherly correction and have matured in my faith. I have openly hashed out doubts, anger, frustrations, and problems too big for myself while walking side by side with Jesus. I have spoken colorfully and candidly with Him about loss. Just as my anger did not scare Him away while in the throes of miscarriage, nothing is too messy for Him. He simply keeps walking alongside me through all of life's crazy days.

When I walk too quickly ahead of Him and eventually tire from the rush, His pace stays steadily the same. When I fall behind in laziness and exhaustion, He patiently extends His hand to help me catch up. All the while, He sings songs of deliverance that wrap around me as a garment while seeing me through every situation. It is here more space is afforded for gratitude to fill my senses to the brim. Oh, how sweet it is.

I hear something beautiful
when you laugh
it is a song declaring
loss did not defeat
and a realization
there is so much joy
hidden among the weeds

Chapter 20

Upward

Last summer, I stood near the moonflowers Addie and I planted while giving them a big gulp of water before the heat of the day set in. Looking closely at the details of the vibrant green vines, I was amazed at how quickly they had wrapped around the trellis near the planted seeds. Twisting and turning, the vines tightly wove themselves upward past the tippy top of the metal support we provided. What a sculpture the vines had created!

While moonflowers can still grow without a trellis system available, they do not flourish and bloom to their full potential without it. Their vines were created to grab onto a sturdy support system. They were made to twirl and stretch upward foot after foot. They weren't intended to become ground cover lacking in blooms; they were made to move upward.

As I peered closely at the moonflowers Addie and I planted, I noticed the vines had wrapped their arms so tightly around our trellis that it appeared as if the two had become one. I had to move the leaves and sleeping blooms aside to even see the trellis hidden underneath. It was as though the support had become a bone structure for the growing vines. As I took note of all of this, a set of verses came to mind from Jesus' teachings as recorded in the book of John.

"Remain in me, and I will remain in you. For a branch cannot produce fruit if it is severed from the vine, and you cannot be fruitful unless you remain in me. Yes, I am the vine; you are the branches. Those who remain in me, and I in them, will produce much fruit. For apart from me you can do nothing" (John 15:4-5 NLT).

While moonflowers are not grapevines (Jesus' analogy of choice in this passage), a similar concept was visually laid out before me. If Jesus was to be represented in my view of the moonflowers, He would obviously be the trellis, the support, the "bones." And if I am the moonflower, I would long to be tightly woven around that anchoring support He provides. The vine and trellis remain together, and I long to remain planted and flourishing next to Jesus. Apart from the trellis, the moonflower does not fully thrive as intended. Likewise, apart from Jesus, I am not provided the strength and support I need to become all I was created to be. In addition, if the moonflower vines were ever ripped away from its trellis, such an act would be detrimental to the life and purpose of the blooms. If I were to untangle my arms from Jesus, the same would happen to me.

I see this concept as foundational in my own life. We live in a world that shouts, "Speak your own truth! You are strong enough on your own! Look deep inside yourself, follow your own path, and you will find you are all you need!" However, I have tested and tried these beliefs—my own beliefs—and found them to be quite temporary and incomplete. While I may have bursts of growth I credit to myself, in actuality, my strength only exists because God is gracious, compassionate, and incredibly forgiving. My own personal truth can cause me to grow, but only sideways like unfruitful, invasive ground cover. In contrast, the truth of God and His immutable Word is one that I will forsake my own opinions for and cling to as if they are a strong trellis in which I can weave around and around until He and I are no longer independently decipherable. God's character is the sole source of strength and support on which I grow.

Some would argue this is indeed "my truth," but it is not. I have met my own truth born of my fickle, fleshy feelings. My own truth is self-centered and God-blaming. My own truth tricks me into thinking my thoughts and desires ought to be of greater value than His. My own truth rewrites Scripture to match my opinions and causes me to take quick offense. My own truth sees life through a temporal lens and leaves me lacking. My own truth does not leave any space for renaming struggles and causes my emotions to reign as conceitedly supreme. However, I resign this way of living because I have explored its terrain and found no lasting freedom or healing among all the quicksand and selfish mirages of "my truth."

In light of this, I have adopted Jesus' truth: *"Remain in me, and I will remain in you."* This tells me I do not have to live life on my own and teaches me I am to be grafted into the larger vine that is Christ Himself. This shows me His truth is better than mine. As I ingest His Word, seek to intimately know Him, and learn the sound of His voice, His truth begins coursing through my veins. His truth has constantly become the life-giving, gratitude-laden infusion that I need afresh every day.

Why has this been so foundational in my life? Because my own truth didn't come with an invitation to see life with a greater appreciation after my losses, nor did it soothe the gaping wounds inside my soul. His did. My truth didn't have the power to bring our babies back from the dead, but God's truth holds them in His arms. Seeing life through this vantage point has deepened who I am as a human being. Feeling His great love for me so tangibly through various circumstances has caused me to love others, myself, and life itself on a whole new level. I see what I was previously too blinded to notice. His truth has made me a new creation. What a great, generous grace this is.

While trying to define what healing after loss looks like is nearly impossible with its individualistic complexities, it is Jesus who stretches out His arm of support as He invites all of us to trust and follow Him through everything we face. He meets us in our shifting circumstances, sees our individualistic pain, and offers the truth of His kindness and grace as a support for us to cling to. It is here our own paths to healing are not "our own truths," but unique, overflowing responses to His goodness. We are all given the invitation to become branches grafted into the ultimate, nourishing vine. Or, as in the analogy of the moonflower, we are given the opportunity to cling to a stronger support system than what our limitations afford us. That support is God, the Author and Creator of everything and the source of unlimited strength.

Grief will never stop its attempts to rip us from the support of who God is. It will never stop telling us God is incapable and unloving. It will always make us feel as though we are abandoned. This is not the truth. This is not YOUR truth. Stop listening to the voice of grief and perceive this: God has not gone anywhere, despite what your feelings might say. He is the support system that is right next to you, even if it is too dark to see. Reach and call out to Him. You did not create God, so you cannot redefine who He says He is. Grief cannot unseat His promises. He will never leave you or forsake you (Deuteronomy 31:8). Wrap yourself around Him, for He is the way, the truth, and the life (John 14:6). Other truths will come and go like the shifting of the wind, but His is the only truth strong enough to forever remain.

wouldn't it be beautiful
if statues were constructed
of ordinary people
and plaques were written
about commonplace situations
because it all happened
and it all mattered
and the unpretentious
is so very sacred

so I will love richly
notice freely
and everything ordinary
will be celebrated
as monumental
and astounding

my bones
have been soaked
in sorrow
I have tasted
rot and poison
yet here
drenched in starlight
I am still standing
eyes wide open
deeply breathing

Chapter 21

But Now I See

My eyesight has been fairly decent for most of my life—20/20, to be precise. So a few months ago, when I started noticing highway signs becoming more difficult to read, I thought I was simply collecting extra floaty bits in my eyes. Call it ignorance, but I started frequently rubbing my eyes, thinking that would somehow clear up my vision. As it turns out, I simply needed glasses.

When the optometrist set my new pair of glasses upon my face, I blinked a few times and began to laugh. Seriously? The world was this crisp and clear? My eyesight had been changing so very slowly over the course of time that I had come to believe my fuzzy-edged world was normal. Yes, highway signs were now much easier to read with my new glasses seated upon my nose, but I could not believe the other various details I had been missing. Individual leaves on distant trees were now distinguishable. Birds perched on tapestries of telephone lines were filled with feathered detail. Even the night sky held a seemingly crisper collection of stars. Everything vibrated with newfound clarity. While I had not realized time caused my eyesight to change, I was now given the chance to see with newfound clarity. While I am no longer the proud owner of perfect vision, I have a tool to help me see all the details of life. Now fully realizing the haze I was formerly living in, I am extra grateful for these new glasses of mine. And goodness, the world is certainly full of beautiful things to see.

I feel as though loss has done the same, but in a spiritual sense. Loss has helped me see tiny details previously unnoticed. It has become an instrument of clarity and of more precise vision. It has become a conduit of gratitude. Grief has opened my eyes and caused me to live life more awake. It constantly serves as a reminder of just how temporary everything, and every moment, is.

If time itself is anything definable, it's liquid. The days pass by quickly, dripping through fingertips. They slip by like sentences running into one another, like a river of words, experiences, memories, moments, and feelings floating downstream in a constant, steady motion. And like trying to hold river current in my palms, loss has caused me to quickly realize the moments I'm generously given are not mine to keep. Prior to feeling the breaking ache of loss, I knew in my mind how temporary and sweet life was, but I didn't fully realize it. I did not *feel* the dire need to squeeze every drop of goodness from my days. My eyes were focused on myself and my own selfish desires and dramas, not the beautifully intricate world surrounding me.

Just like setting my new glasses upon my nose and noticing all the crisp details surrounding me, loss woke me up to the fact that this life is quickly fleeting. If I'm not digging deep into my days to unearth all the beautiful details found in the wonderful, the ugly, and all the mundane, I am wasting what has been given to me. Realizing this truth was like dusting off a buried gem. One does not have to feel rosy and perfectly happy to notice what is good; it can still occur while feeling the heaviness of disappointment and grief. As previously stated, such things can co-exist.

The moment I decided to set down the draining pursuit of chasing after what I did not have, my vision became crisper. The moment I decided to shift my gaze away from the empty portions of my life, I saw the abundance sitting before me like a delicious feast waiting to be savored. The daily decision to focus my eyes and my heart on what is gloriously present has not filled me with things I can keep forever, but it has satisfied my longing to live a fuller life.

Yes, in my hands I have literally held broken pieces of my heart in the form of our little, tiny babies who did not survive. As traumatic as that was, it did not detract from the fact that our babies were incredibly beautiful—remarkable beings I have clutched in my hands—and then had to let go. Like everything else I have felt. Like everyone else I have held. So what, then, can I do to constantly feel the moments of my life and notice the beauty in this ever-changing, temporary world? I can *decide* to live with eyes wide open, like I'm seeing everything new for the very first time over and over again.

Have you ever experienced a moment that caused you to pause and drink it in while committing all the details to memory? And before that moment dissolved into the next, have you picked it apart to save the layers like photographs hung in the halls of your mind? I am certain we have all had times such as these, where we truly appreciate the seconds before they swish by. But what if we did this more often? What if we truly savored the flavors of the here and now before they become mere aftertastes? This is living with eyes wide open, and it truly is a conscious decision leading to appreciating not only the perfectly bright blue sunny days that come, but also the dark nights where more focus of sight is necessary.

A few years ago, I asked Addie a question as I was tucking her into bed at night. I asked, "What small, tiny things are you thankful for right now?" She tilted her head, as if surprised by the question, but after a few seconds I saw a light flicker across her imaginative eyes.

"Like, the things that we normally don't pay much attention to?" she inquired back.

"Yes. For instance, I noticed the way my violin felt underneath my fingers as I played it today. I could feel the strings buzzing with vibration and it made me smile to feel the music and not just hear it. I saw a small cloud of rosin rise when my bow dragged across the strings, and it made me happy to see the effects of the music I was playing... Like that. What's something you normally wouldn't pay attention to that you're thankful for?"

After a small pause to gather thoughts, we began to talk slowly at first, then all at once, as if embers had grown into flame. We spoke of muted moonlight and the smoldering stars peeking through our trees. We noticed the scent of post-dinner cherry pie still hanging sweetly in the air. We smiled at the sound of my husband, Kirk's laughter floating down the hall and the feel of our dog's soft, blonde fur on our fingers while petting her as she snored at our feet. We discussed the wonder of the late summer night's chill, and how our breath hung like ghosts in midair. We laughed as we remembered the quick wit and humor of our friends and the belly laughter shared together over lunch earlier in the day. We discussed the sense of accomplishment that comes with mastering a new set of notes on a page. We gave thanks for the taste of the hot chocolate and tea we drank while watching the sunset on the back patio prior to bedtime.

And oh! Sunsets! We both love to adore the wide-open country sky when dusk gathers slowly and unfurls into soft lavenders and deep blues. We spoke of God's paintbrush and His ability to transform colors with just one wisp of His brushstroke. The ancient sky is the same canvas that has always been since the beginning of creation, but the paintings never remain the same. The movement of a sunset is repeated every day, but it never looks the same. THAT, we decided, is something we are grateful to witness. We looked into each other's smiling eyes, and as we continued our conversation, we marveled at how being right there together in that small blip of time was its own miraculous wonder.

Soon enough, Addie's eyes grew heavy and I tucked her beneath the covers. Before I closed her door, she sweetly asked, "Mom, can we do this every night? I want to challenge myself to notice all the small things in my day and then talk about them with you." After I mopped my melted heart off the floor, I promised her we most definitely would. I was certainly okay with our bedtime routine growing in length and sweetness all in one.

Later in the evening, as I prepared to drift off to sleep and say goodbye to another day, I thought about how fulfillment truly is found by simply noticing all the small things that comprise our days. Perhaps life's deepest joys are not found in the "looking forward to" or "longing for" but are instead hidden in plain view right here in the ever-changing present and seemingly mundane. Noticing them is like placing a fresh pair of much-needed glasses upon the soul.

Could I have learned the depth of this lesson without loss? To some extent, yes. But without loss, I would not see the full value of the mundane. I would not fully perceive the abundance sitting right in front of me. And perhaps I would not be as filled to the brim with gratitude while fully understanding all the wonders of today are but a passing blink.

in the shade of an ancient oak
cooled breeze slips across my face

I watch light dance and drizzle
through clusters of sun-soaked leaves

a sliver of bright drips into my open palm

I roll it
and poke it
until it spills
all over the place

Chapter 22

Unearthing Treasure

Kirk, Addie, and I don't get too many opportunities to enjoy time away together. Ministry life is abundant, and often family vacations move to the back burner. In fact, any travel opportunities that come our way are usually in the form of mission work and not for simple pleasure. However, after several years of not taking a break to rest together, we knew it was time. It is necessary and healthy to press "pause" on regular life from time to time, and we decided we needed to create more space for such. Addie was about to enter high school, after all, and her time with us at home was quickly fleeting.

Soon enough, the three of us found ourselves driving through Alaska, and I was quickly rendered speechless by the beauty surrounding us. While I had seen beautiful places in the world, it all paled in comparison to the buffet for the senses wrapping around us. As we drove into Valdez, a small coastal town on the Prince William Sound, I asked out loud, "IS THIS EVEN REAL?"

It looked as though we were driving into an AI-generated movie scene or a different universe entirely. Mist hovered and danced slowly while weaving through elevated passes. Mountains both stretched high and sloped low as though melting into ocean water while patches of fog floated like brush strokes across the horizon. The thickest rainbow I have ever laid eyes upon connected clouds to water, and I was overcome. I felt as though I was ingesting more dessert than I could handle, and when it came time to go to sleep that evening, I sat awake overstuffed with delight. There were no adequate words to describe the scenes we witnessed, and no pictures could be taken to correctly convey the reality of it all. Such things simply had to be *felt*. If I had a thousand lifetimes at my disposal, it still would not be enough time to explore every inch of beauty hidden in those mountainsides. And if a million new words were added to language, I am certain none could begin to truly describe the wonder of *feeling* the landscape.

Valdez is known for its numerous waterfalls, and while only a few are named, there are countless more in existence. As we continued driving around to explore, I noticed a crevice in a far-off mountainside. An unnamed waterfall was tucked deeply into towering rock, practically hidden from the view of those driving past on the road. If a passerby did not squint and zero in on the crack in the vast mountain range, it would never be noticed. Far fewer would hike through the bear-laden woods to hear the sound of its waters shattering against rocks and feel its cool mist upon skin.

Noticing that hidden waterfall opened my eyes wider to see a character trait found in our Creator: He makes so many wonders simply for the joy of it. He creates without demanding attention, knowing full well many of us will never have the capacity to notice and appreciate all the details He places in creation. A waterfall hidden deep in the Alaskan wilderness, a fleck of sky-blue hidden in an otherwise brown eye, the iridescent sheen of a fish swimming in ocean depths, the vein of a leaf growing high up in a tree, the moonflower that unfurls when the sun is hidden from sight... things such as these are largely grazed over by the average busybody. There are so many details God placed in creation that it would be impossible to notice them all.

AND YET He creates with the most skilled, attentive detail just because that is who He is. When it comes to our own bodies, the same is true. He did not hold back one ounce of attentiveness when He created us. To think of all the variations found in our strands of DNA (and how each one of us is completely unique) is awe-inspiring. There are so many details hidden on and inside our bodies we will never fully realize or appreciate. From fingerprints to skin shade, hair color to face shape, mannerisms and personality characteristics, many spend their lifetime focusing on what they deem as flawed in their bodies instead of noticing the sheer miraculous amount of God's creativity written upon their DNA. To remove or change such things would be an attempt to erase the intriguing handiwork of God Himself. He creates each one of us with joy, even though so many of us do not see it.

Psalm 139:13-18 (NLT) says, *"You made all the delicate, inner parts of my body and knit me together in my mother's womb. Thank you for making me so wonderfully complex! Your workmanship is marvelous—how well I know it. You watched me as I was being formed in utter seclusion, as I was woven together in the dark of the womb. You saw me before I was born. Every day of my life was recorded in your book. Every moment was laid out before a single day had passed. How precious are your thoughts about me, O God. They cannot be numbered! I can't even count them; they outnumber the grains of sand! And when I wake up, you are still with me!"*

You and I are not here because of some off-chance accident, nor are we here because we are God's botched experiment. We were created as an overflow of God's careful, wonderful attentiveness. He created us out of sheer delight and intent. I often forget this. I have wasted an embarrassing amount of time with magnifying glass in hand inspecting the parts of me I am displeased with. If I had been able to sculpt myself, I would have made some adjustments, both big and small. I have often forgotten I am fearfully and wonderfully made. I have easily dismissed the idea that my unique features are what make me who I am.

But the mountains do not wish to be smaller. The waterfalls do not wish to be grander. The birds do not ask to trade feathers with one another. The snowflakes do not envy each other. How sad it would make all of us if that were true. Instead, they simply are who the Creator says they are—full of magnificent, unique detail. No two things in creation are exactly alike, and everything exists to point to God's astounding majesty. Including me. Including you. Including our life stories.

As I spent unhurried time watching the mist dance around mountaintops, I thought about these truths. I repented for the discontent I had elevated onto a pedestal in my life. I praised the God who fearfully, wonderfully, joyfully, and constantly creates. His skill is unmatched. His eye for detail is unrivaled. His ability is unsurpassed. No loss, gain, joy, or pain is lost under His detail-oriented gaze.

moonflowers do not need convincing
to unfold under a blanket
of star-speckled blue

they do not doubt their purpose
fret over provision
nor waste their brief moments
on concern or comparison

they do not apologize
for emerging
when it is their time
they simply know
who they are
in this brief, brilliant moment
and bravely bloom
in the silence of night

you are sacred architecture
more than stardust and chance
what a series of miracles
it took for you to exist

(you are an exquisite work of art)

Chapter 23

Pruning

Moonflowers can easily become little troublemakers, as they are often known to take over the gardens they are planted into. If left to their own devices without the attentive care of a gardener, they are very likely to choke out surrounding plants.[1] In addition, if left unpruned, their leafy vines can become more plentiful than their actual moon-like blooms. Quite simply stated, for these flowers to remain as healthy as possible, they must be clipped and pruned at least a few times during their blooming season.

For us to remain healthy and blooming, we must go through our own pruning processes not just once, but constantly. Jesus says in John 15:1-3 (NLT), *"I am the true grapevine, and my Father is the gardener. He cuts off every branch of mine that doesn't produce fruit, and he prunes the branches that do bear fruit so they will produce even more. You have already been pruned and purified by the message I have given you."*

While this verse refers to actual *people* being pruned off the grapevine branches by God, it does show us the importance of vine maintenance. For grapevines to remain healthy while yielding bountiful amounts of fruit, unproductive branches must be removed. For the moonflowers to remain in-check and blooming, excess vines must be trimmed. For the body of Christ (the church) to remain well-functioning, destructive and unproductive members must be removed. Likewise, for our own souls to fully flourish, we must allow the Great Gardener of Souls to prune off pieces of our lives that hinder what He longs to accomplish in us.

Through our very human experiences, we can begin to bloom in unexpected ways as we latch on to Jesus, yet still easily begin growing chutes of anxiety, anger, doubt, worry, jealousy, discontent, and selfishness, among so many other things. This is why we need Him consistently. As the old hymn says, "Lord, I need Thee, every hour I need Thee." How true this is. As we unfold and bloom, we constantly need God to search us, know us, and daily remove every part of us that would hinder our growth.

While we are quick to grow harmful characteristics that require persistent removal, there are also seemingly "good" vines that, upon deeper scrutiny from the Almighty, are useless to our growth. Sometimes harmful elements appear to be full of life, and we have difficulty deciphering between what holds death and what leads to growth on our own. This is why we need God to identify such things and help us lop off pieces that hinder His work in our lives.

This means we need our Gardener to be present with us in every moment. We need His presence without our resistance. We need a great measure of humility as we allow Him to search and KNOW us; and we need to selflessly allow Him to remove what would otherwise lead to disease and stunted growth, even if such things hold the appearance of good.

The moonflowers do not get to choose whether they are pruned or not, but our own pruning processes require our participation. More so, our active surrender is needed. God, in all His sovereignty, can do whatever He pleases, and oftentimes it may feel as though He is the scissor-happy gardener forcefully removing pieces from us without explanation. While He can do this, if we take a step back, we better realize He is a gentle gardener full of intent. Each piece that He longs to prune off is done so with a greater picture of eventual health in mind. And many times, it requires our active obedience, participation, and surrender to allow this pruning to happen.

Pruning is rarely comfortable or easy, but it is a holy process. It is trusting the One who can bring us to a place of health and continual growth. It's allowing Him to refine us by removing what should not stay. It's trading what seems good for what is eternally better. It is a holy, active, constant surrender.

Part Three
Surrender

grief is an unfastening
of every belief
this world holds power
to gift us "forever"

Chapter 24

Release

Just as sunsets blaze into the horizon with brilliant, awe-inspiring shades of wonder, autumn's fiery hues remind us that endings can be gloriously beautiful. If sunsets and autumns never came, this world would be incomplete. We would forever be in the holding pattern of daylight and summertime. But here's the thing: just as waves and feelings never go away, but only transform, the endings found inside sunsets and autumns signify "change" more than "death." They don't exist to merely signify endings but to usher in new beginnings. Sunsets give way to starry nights, and the mouth of dawn opens to reveal new light once again. Blazing autumns surrender to frozen winters, but the much-anticipated thaw of spring always breaks through the chill.

It is here in late autumn the moonflowers begin to grow weary after their brilliant moments of summer-sweet bloom. However, they are not merely in a shriveling, drying, and dying process but are gracefully preparing for more life. While they begin shifting in response to the newly chilled season, they also create little-seeded legacies packaged within wooden pods. As blossoms begin to bow their heads for a final time, these intricately-shaped pods grow pregnant with hope and new possibility. This process of letting go is not the final say. It is necessary for new life to flourish once again. This wilting does not proclaim, "THE END," but rather, "WAIT! THERE IS MORE!"

I know all too well when something beloved ends, and when someone cherished dies, it leaves abundant painful feelings behind. I am not naturally eager to call such endings beautiful, nor do I ever wish to experience them. However, when viewing these experiences in the light of eternity, I begin to see they are necessary in this life. Such painful processes give way to what's next. They are transitions. Nothing here lasts forever, and none of us are created to live in this place for all eternity. Death and loss are merely a yielding to more... to *heaven*. *Eternity*. A place beyond our wildest imaginations. A place where there are no more painful goodbyes, teary heartbreaks, or disappointing endings.

These autumnal seasons of our lives here on earth—the moments of necessary surrender—can be so incredibly rich and bring about freedom-infused, abundant life with enough sustainability to stretch beyond the temporal here and now. Surrender aches, and many times it outright stings. At times it even feels like a deeply terrifying leap into the unknown. However, surrender is not a solo freefall into a man-eating abyss. Instead, it is a trust fall into very capable arms. It is not the end but an invitation to *more*.

afternoon light
curls around fingertips
casting shadows
upon the wall
I try to hold it steady
but it keeps moving
shifting
changing
so I keep feeling warmth
wrap around my skin
and then
I let it go

Chapter 25

Open Hands

"Every time I tried clinging on to something too tightly, it still found a way to slip through my hands. So I don't cling to anything but God anymore" (Alma Foth, most affectionately known as "Oma").

These simple words of wisdom were shared by my Oma (the German name for grandma) over warm, homemade pierogies in her cozy upstairs apartment on a crisp, fall afternoon. Pierogies do not take minutes or hours to make, but days. This meal was a labor of love to feed the bellies of those whom my Oma loves.

Not much in my Oma's life has come easily, and if anyone is ever qualified to give advice, it is her. Having grown up in Poland as a full-blooded German, the start of World War II brought turmoil right to her doorstep. She and her family were hated by the people of Poland simply because of their German blood, so she and her sisters were sent to various Polish work camps during the war. Conditions were awful, and by the time the war ended, she had been starved, raped, robbed of family members, and spit out as a refugee with no home in which to return. The process of immigrating to America and starting a new life was long and difficult; and having now become a new wife and mother while living as a refugee in Germany after the war, she and my Opa (grandpa) had to cross an ocean on a cargo ship with two toddlers in tow. Once finally settled into a foreign land and learning a new language, she suffered the pain of miscarriage. And years later, she would be faced with the task of burying both her son (my Uncle Norb) as well as her husband.

Loss, poverty, and difficulty had riddled her life, yet here she was, generously sharing hard-earned wisdom over a rich meal. Like a resilient moonflower, she kept blooming again and again, even when her dark circumstances threatened to crush her core. How does one survive such difficulty? The obvious answers would include words like "strength," "tenacity," and "determination," but the secret shared around the table that day was this: live with your hands wide open. "God has been constantly teaching me I cannot hold too tightly to all these things that don't last," she said, "and every time I try to cling on to temporary people and things, He shows me once again that I cannot keep anything in this life except for Him."

Living with open hands means freedom from trying to own it all, be it all, prove it all, and figure everything out. It means caring deeply but not frantically clinging to that which ends. It means surviving loss and weathering storms with joy still intact. It is understanding that everything in this life is fluid, constantly undergoing currents of change and motion. Open hands keep us from lashing out in anger when situations do not go our way and frees us from plagues of over-thinking and over-lingering. We would be kept from a haughty attitude of self-entitlement if we adopted this way of living.

Deciding to experience life with fingers and palms unclenched could also alter the way we view ourselves. We would be quicker to forgive our many faults, understanding though we will let ourselves down often, we are still worthy of grace. Open-handed living would bring more humble confidence, less dwelling on the past, and less focus on the uncontrollable future. Worry would have to flee because there would simply be no space for it. We would be less selfish and more abundant with wonder. Instead of focusing internally, we would be free to notice, love, and wonder without claiming ownership and control. Our hands would be rid of so many negative aspects we constantly insist upon holding.

As I listened to my Oma share wisdom in her apartment that day, I was, and still am, reminded of "The Cure for Anxiety" found in Luke 12:22-34 (NLT):

> "Then, turning to his disciples, Jesus said, 'That is why I tell you not to worry about everyday life—whether you have enough food to eat or enough clothes to wear. For life is more than food, and your body more than clothing. Look at the ravens. They don't plant or harvest or store food in barns, for God feeds them. And you are far more valuable to him than any birds! Can all your worries add a single moment to your life? And if worry can't accomplish a little thing like that, what's the use of worrying over bigger things?
>
> "'Look at the lilies and how they grow. They don't work or make their clothing, yet Solomon in all his glory was not dressed as beautifully as they are. And if God cares so wonderfully for flowers that are here today and thrown into the fire tomorrow, he will certainly care for you. Why do you have so little faith? And don't be concerned about what to eat and what to drink. Don't worry about such things. These things dominate the thoughts of unbelievers all over the world, but your Father already knows your needs. Seek the Kingdom of God above all else, and he will give you everything you need.
>
> "'So don't be afraid, little flock. For it gives your Father great happiness to give you the Kingdom. Sell your possessions and give to those in need. This will store up treasure for you in heaven! And

the purses of heaven never get old or develop holes. Your treasure will be safe; no thief can steal it and no moth can destroy it. Wherever your treasure is, there the desires of your heart will also be.'"

Day by day (often moment by moment), I am learning the rich truths found in these verses. It is easier said than done, to continually unclench fists. But goodness, it is incredibly tiring to constantly hold so tightly to everything that is not designed to stay. There has to be an alternative to such laborious living. There *is* an alternative. Jesus even explains to us how to go about it in His Word: do not worry, consider the perfect provision of our heavenly Father, seek His kingdom over earthly possessions, do not be afraid, and store up treasure that will last in heaven. He calls us to open-handed, heavenly-kingdom-minded living. This is not simply a suggestion for us to apply only if we feel like doing so. It is a manual for experiencing life to the fullest extent.

If my Oma learned how to live out these truths, I am certain we can, too. She is not superhuman, and age has not made her immune to the sting of loss. In fact, as time goes on, we all naturally become more susceptible to it. Her wisdom did not come through a life painted with the perfection found in an endless well of her own desires coming to pass. Instead, it was steadily built through applying the truth of God's Word in times of plenty, seasons of heartache, blissful experiences, and awful grief. She is one of the most beautiful people I know because she lives unabashedly surrendered to her Savior, no matter what has come her way. The only One she now clings to is Him, and Him alone.

As I sat at her table that day, I thought of all the miracles that brought us all to that moment. There had been a literal war, homelessness, settling in an unknown country, learning a new language, enduring much hardship, and losing more than I will ever comprehend. But there had also been so much gain

—an immeasurable amount of bravery, adventure, trust, joy, generosity, wisdom, strength, and a legacy of love stretching through generations. Nothing was wasted, and it all brought us to that moment as we shared a meal together.

Her open hands meant there was room enough for me to enter the current of faith in the God who saw her through everything. Oma's surrender is both a demonstration and an invitation. Her life is like a collection of psalms singing of His faithfulness through the deepest nights and the brightest days. She has steadfastly demonstrated a life wrapped tightly around Jesus instead of circumstance, and she invites me to do the same; but just as anything deeply meaningful, this did not come easy. A legacy such as this is not created through microwaved circumstance but through slow-roasted experience. Perhaps this is why she always chose to make us tediously delicious pierogies. They take time to take shape… days of work occur in order to spread such a meal across the table. She always knew true nutrition takes time. And a lifetime of learning how to surrender and submit to God's hand—that brings about lasting nourishment at its finest.

if any earthly thing
is to remain spectacular
I cannot call it
mine

Chapter 26

Surrender and Submission

Oh, but surrender is so difficult, isn't it? When I imagine surrender, the first thing that comes to mind is an army terribly surrounded. A white flag is raised, weapons fall to the ground, and arms lift to the sky. Surrender, in this context, is undesired. It is a realization that previous plans have been foiled.

According to *dictionary.com*, surrender is a "cease of resistance to an enemy or opponent in order to submit to their authority." And submission? Submission is "to accept or yield to a superior force or to the authority and will of another." First, there must be a ceasing of resistance. Then, there must be a yielding to an authority that is not ours. These concepts go against our selfish desires, don't they? While nature itself has no hesitation in the surrender of summer into autumn, golden hour into nightfall, and moonflower bloom into seedpod, it is a different story for us. Humankind largely fights against surrender and submission. We war against it. We only desire change if it comfortably matches our definitions of agreeable living, and we do not appreciate, nor easily trust, any outside authority that might lead us in a different direction. And yet

Surrender and Submission

Scripture tells us offering ourselves as living sacrifices to God and becoming transformed by the renewing of our mind are both necessary for true and proper worship (Romans 12:1-2).

While there are no Bible verses that explicitly use the command "surrender to God," there are references that explain to us the necessity of "ceasing our resistance" to Him. For example, in Matthew 16:24 (NLT), Jesus says to His disciples, *"If any of you wants to be my follower, you must give up your own way, take up your cross, and follow me."* Additionally, Paul states in Galatians 2:20 (NLT), *"My old self has been crucified with Christ. It is no longer I who live, but Christ lives in me. So I live in this earthly body by trusting in the Son of God, who loved me and gave himself for me."* Then, James 4:7 (NIV) gives the command to *"Submit yourselves, then, to God."*

For the Christ follower, surrender and submission are required. We must cease our resistance to the God who knows the full-framed picture of our lives, and then we must yield to His will even if it is uncomfortable, doesn't make sense, and hurts in the temporary. Why? Because, as Romans 8:28 (NLT) tells us, *"And we know that God causes everything to work together for the good of those who love God and are called according to his purpose for them."* While suffering, pain, loss, and discomfort may not have been a part of God's original plan for humanity, the fallen state of our temporary world includes such things. However, even through difficulty, God has a plan.

Undesirable circumstances can be used to perfect our faith and make us better see that the character of God is a stark contrast to all our pain. Through trials, we not only hear about His nearness, but we experience it. We not only learn about His character, but we realize His beautiful layers. We not only read about His promises, but we live them firsthand. He works all things together for the good of those who love Him, even if circumstances don't appear "good" at first glance or make perfect sense to us in the moment.

However, if I were to honestly evaluate how I have often approached life, it would be this: my life is a continual cycle of trying to keep people, things, and circumstances that are not mine. It is a pattern of surrendering and submitting, then doubting, backpedaling, and attempting to once again cling to the temporary. Living in open-handed surrender sounds like an attractively easy process on paper, but it doesn't take a genius to quickly realize the actual act is immeasurably more cumbersome in practice. Listening to my Oma talk about living without gripping tightly to all that is not God is easy to hear but difficult to duplicate. Highlighting Scripture in my Bible that teaches me to submit to God is easy, but living it out is incredibly arduous. As already pointed out, human nature wars against such things. It is in my human nature to war against an authority that does not originate from my own self.

I have been given the invitation to surrender, submit, and live with hands open, but I often decline because these things require patience and self-denial. Because I am naturally selfish, surrender and submission are hard-earned lessons that often involve failure. While I desire to loosen my grip from that which is temporary, I often find myself feeling as though I am entitled to things that will never have my name on it. I so easily forget this existence of mine is fleeting. In actuality, surrender is often so very hard. In reality, submission is a sacrifice. And I believe both are so difficult because my line of sight is limited by the boundaries of time. I cannot see heaven with my natural eyes. I cannot truly perceive the value of eternity because I am surrounded by impermanent. In fact, that is which is impermanent often seems to be of greatest value because that is all I can see with my natural eyes. While situations scream in my face and cloud my vision, eternity is a contrast that must be gently perceived.

For as often as we fail, there are continual invitations given to live in surrender and submission to Christ. There is grace

Surrender and Submission

upon grace through every situation. If we are to truly live robustly, we need to surrender and submit to the One who is working all things for the good, even when we don't yet understand or fully see. When we fall short and try to cling to what we think we will stay forever, or if we try to take control and work things for our own good without God's assistance, we will find His hand is still there. It is always extended to us. It's always inviting us to let go of what we think we own and instead surrender and submit to His capable authorship. Even when the here and now hurts terribly, there is always an opportunity to trust Him more.

Isaiah 41:10 (NLT) says, *"Don't be afraid, for I am with you. Don't be discouraged, for I am your God. I will strengthen you and help you. I will hold you up with my victorious right hand."* The Lord is a mighty sustainer for all of us. When we surrender and submit, we learn what it is to trust this truth. We give Him the opportunity to show Himself faithful. We begin to reassign value to what we see before us and place it upon that which is eternal. It is up to us, then, to open our hands, lay down our defenses, and trust that He is not our opponent demanding surrender and submission, but our capable authority who deserves our yielding. This process of continually re-opening our hands, surrendering our plans, and submitting to the One who is infinitely wise is birthed in the decision to be thankful no matter the circumstance.

Pastor Tom, a close friend and coworker of mine, showed me firsthand how such a concept can be lived out. Amid struggles he was facing, he simply smiled, shook his head, and said, "Well, praise God!" The challenging situations before him were incredibly overwhelming. If he had broken down into a puddle of tears and had a full-blown panic attack, I would have completely understood. However, that was not his response. Instead, he said, "There's so much going wrong, God has to be working in all of this. So I'm praising God for all of it because these are just opportunities for me to see Him at work and to know more about who He is."

His attitude quickly became contagious. "Praise God" has become a knee-jerk response among our staff and many of our church members not just when life is rosy, but when things go ridiculously wrong. We may not always initially *feel* like praising God and thanking Him for our circumstances when jobs are lost, bills are overdue, sickness is present, family members are difficult, or even when we face death and grief, but doing so is living out 1 Thessalonians 5:16-18 (NIV). *"Rejoice always,"* it reads. *"...pray continually, give thanks in all circumstances; for this is God's will for you in Christ Jesus."*

Saying "praise God" puts the mouth and mind in position for the heart to see more clearly. It reorients feelings of panic, fear, and worry and submits them to Christ. It leaves us open to not just the possibility, but the reality that God is at work despite our terrible situations. It leads us to know Him better than we did before. It doesn't override grief but turns our gaze toward the One who is with us and working in and among the worst of the worst. Is this not the very thing Paul and Silas demonstrated for us while prisoners in Acts 16?

Pointing the finger once again at gratitude, this is one of the very best catalysts to living life to the full. No one is exempt from the power of thankfulness, no matter the current life station. Even horrors such as war, violence, abuse, poverty, discrimination, and beyond do not veto the ability to choose gratitude because God never stops working despite it all. You might call me idealistic or ignorant in my limited worldview, but 1 Thessalonians does not say, "Give thanks in some situations." Instead, it says, "Give thanks in ALL situations." Everyone, everywhere, every time.

Gratitude, at its very core, prepares our hearts and minds for surrender and submission. Gratefulness leads to true and lasting worship, no matter the surrounding night seasons of our lives. It clears the dust of circumstance from our temporal vision and allows us to see through eyes fixed upon eternity.

Think about your own life and current situations. What if you said "praise God" when your situations would normally call for panic, worry, rage, anger, and self-induced control? What if this was the first thing out of your mouth during triggering circumstances? What if, when completely overwhelmed and entirely surrounded, you dropped the weapons held in your own strength, raised your arms in surrender and submission, and declared, "PRAISE GOD!" in the face of your overwhelming pain and intimidating giants?

How entirely subversive. How incredibly pivotal. How rambunctiously rebellious. Aren't you a bit curious how this could change the course of your life?

as sinking light
finishes its song
and twilight
begins to sing along
I see how beautiful it is
to open my hands
and set free
all these pieces
that never
belonged to me

Chapter 27

Amy

In the cool of autumn, gardeners must care for current moonflower vines, blooms, and the beds in which they were planted in order to preserve the hope for next season's health. Moonflowers cannot be left to their own devices. If so, as leaves crisp and dry, blossoms would become scarce. Seedpods would begin falling onto soil, self-seeding would begin to take place, and vines would soon take over. Current and future plants would become wildly unkempt.

In short, what was intended for beauty would turn into a chaotic mess. Moonflowers must be continually pruned, and for the best hope for next year's garden, seedpods must be plucked, collected, and prepared for the future. Self-seeding most assuredly is an option, but in most cases, it is not the best choice for maintaining a beautiful garden. In the hands of a skilled gardener, however, seeds can be properly cared for while in preparation for next season's planting. The garden can be kept clean and impeccable while future seeds are safely stored during the cold months. Then, when the time comes, gardeners can nick, soak, and plant new seeds. A cycle. A process. And for best results, the gardener is present for it all.

Why, then, is it a surprise when our Great Gardener plucks us? If He allowed us to stay in this temporary, flawed existence eternally, we would not remain beautiful. Today's blooms will not stay forever, but with the gardener's help, they can prepare for next season's beauty before they leave. Likewise, God did not design us to live among imperfection forever but helps us prepare for the future glory in which we were truly made to reside. Death is not the end of the story. It clears the way for an eternity ahead.

Surrender. Submission. These are the tools that help us to see death as a doorway, not an end. For the Christ follower, the cruelty of death is for but a moment. *"Death is swallowed up in victory. O death, where is your victory? O death, where is your sting?' For sin is the sting that results in death, and the law gives sin its power. But thank God! He gives us victory over sin and death through our Lord Jesus Christ"* (1 Corinthians 15:54-57 NLT).

The most profound example I have seen firsthand of someone surrendering and submitting in the face of undesirable sickness and death was my dear sister-in-law, Amy. When I first met her, I did not realize just how much of an impact she would make on my life in such a brief period of time. And speaking of time, I did not know I would only have three short years with her. Meeting her was miraculous, sharing life with her was beautiful, and losing her was shattering. But nothing is wasted unless we deliberately waste it. That is why, just as speaking of the losses of our babies, this story is worth telling.

When I first met Amy on an autumn day laced with hazy, low sunlight, I was first taken aback with wonder that she possessed the same exact smile my then-boyfriend Kirk wore every day. She looked SO much like him. As she warmly greeted me with her one-year-old perched upon her hip, I had a feeling she would become one of my very best friends.

That first weekend spent with Amy was filled with morning coffee, slow afternoons, and baby snuggles. Conversation flowed effortlessly over midday cups of tea, and as I listened to the lightness found in her laughter, I realized she was someone I wanted in my life. She was magnetizing. Her genuine love and open arms were like an orbital pull.

From then on, she was there. Once a former stranger, she became family. Mundane moments, significant events, and everything in between were now ours to share. We watched her belly grow with a second baby—another son to love and dote upon. He entered the world with loud, fresh lungs roaring the song of new life, and instantly our smitten hearts made space for more.

In turn, she shared our joy when Kirk asked me to be his bride and stood by my side with her two little boys on that drizzly Saturday I became his wife. A few months later, she packed up her family and made the nine-hour drive to our new home in Michigan. I will never forget how she refused to hold back tears of pride, dabbing red eyes as she listened to my husband—her little brother—preach at our church for the first time.

When we couldn't be together, Amy filled our mailbox with a steady stream of pictures tucked into handwritten letters. Enough to fill an album, she made sure we didn't miss a moment of our nephews' growth. Weekly phone calls allowed us to catch up on details as we chattered about our days. No matter our distance, we filled pages and pages of life stories as we shared the inner workings of our lives.

She was an honest, open book I was freely invited to read and an older sister who gently guided and offered sound advice to aid my young naivety. While Kirk and I were brand new to ministry, she held years of experience in her hands. Because of her time spent serving in youth ministry, she lavished wisdom, gentle direction, and love without judgment or expectation. She was a sounding board, a place of safe security, and a source of sanity as we began our own wild ride of ministry and marriage.

Our time together felt like a guarantee. I assumed we had many years ahead to share together. That is why I believed God would heal and preserve her life when she became very ill only three years after I first met her. Isn't that what we all hope for concerning our loved ones? There is simply no such thing as enough time, and we always plead to God for more. But when it came to Amy, she was the most deserving of a miracle.

Amy had previously been a vibrant, healthy young mom with not a hint of frailty, so we assumed this illness would pass as temporary and manageable. However, as the days went by, mysterious symptoms began to stack upon one another. It quickly became clear something was terribly amiss in her body. One awful October evening, Amy suffered a grand mal seizure that pushed her into a coma. The doctors were both baffled by her mystery illness and unsure she would ever be able to wake again. We packed up our car and sped through all the miles to be by her side. There at her hospital bed, surrounded by the prayers of people from around the world, we watched the miraculous happen. Amy woke up.

Although clearly in pain and far from being alright, we could see her eyes and hear her voice—a beautiful gift. We massaged her legs and spoon fed her hospital cafeteria food as we all tried to make sense of what was happening in her body. While her brain was foggy and her body riddled with ache, we believed in time all would go back to normal. We were tired, concerned, and consumed with trying to understand what was going on in her body, but we held onto hope.

It was here Amy herself exuded the most stunning display of gratitude and trust. She was thankful to be alive in that moment and fully trusted God despite her physical discomfort and unknown future. She surrendered her physical suffering to God while submitting her future to God. As she laid in her ICU hospital bed, Amy asked her husband to play worship music. "If Paul and Silas could worship while they were in prison, I can worship while I'm in pain," she said. Hands lifted while resting in bed, she did just that. She worshiped God even though her circumstances were entirely less than ideal. Her husband watched in awe as she lifted her hands in surrender to God. Her future, no matter what it held, was submitted into the safety of His hands.

What I would deem as "safe" is often bubble-wrapped perfection void of discomfort, pain, and loss. "Be safe!" I say to my loved ones. I don't want to lose any of them. I do not desire for any of us to face difficulties. I don't want things to shift if it means difficult change or loss is included. But God's view of safety is quite different from mine. He sees the entire tapestry while I only see a few threads. He sees beyond the temporary while I cannot. My view of safety seems to include a security that fades. But to God, "safe" means being next to Him, whether in this life or eternity. Therefore, "safe" doesn't necessarily mean *here*. This was realized in the most difficult manner when Amy passed away mere months after her illness first arrived.

I could fill the rest of this book with pages containing the complex feelings we experienced after Amy's death. Deep wells of anger, endless waves of sadness, smiles from shared memories, and feelings of wanting to shut down and hide away, we felt it all. But mostly, we were blindsided with disbelief. Amy left and it wasn't our choice. She was gone. This was the reality we were given. There was no promissory note left behind explaining why we had to make such a payment, and in exchange, we were left with broken hearts and a million question marks. I could write chapter upon chapter complaining about how it simply wasn't fair and didn't make sense to us. Why would God allow a young mother with a beautiful ministry to pass away so quickly? While the world contained a variety of people still healthy, living, and breathing, she wasn't with us any longer. Why her? Why us? *WHY?* Why didn't we see the miracle we were praying for?

As discussed earlier, no answer to "why" could ever suffice. There was no reasoning to soothe our natural feelings. Our sadness, anger, and questions would not bring her back. And while we were, and still are, entitled to feel all the complex feelings surrounding such a painful loss, my mind often wanders back to what Amy chose to do in that hospital bed. She unfolded through surrender and submission. She truly worshiped despite what was happening. She chose to trust. She chose to lay aside her own questions and pain and worshiped even though she didn't know what was ahead.

This is maturity and faith in its grittiest, truest, most significant form. Submitting to God when situations tend toward comfort and favorability is easy. Conversely, submission is quite a difficult decision when circumstances are terrible and it is assumed God is neither good nor trustworthy. But Amy? She chose to deny her own feelings and worship despite. She knew beyond a shadow of a doubt surrendering and submitting to God was wise because He works everything together for the good of those who love Him. She knew this temporary pain would not be the end of her story. Either God would heal her, guide her through the physical challenges, or usher her into eternal paradise. No matter the avenue, all things would work together for her good. Her surrender, submission, and worship set her attitude for what was ahead. No matter what her future would look like, faith prepared her heart.

Though we still wrestle with all the layers of grief left in the wake of her passing, Amy is in eternity. Heaven. The place we were truly designed for. The place with no endings, pain, tears, or goodbyes. The place where gold, the most precious of metal, is used for pavement. The place where God, in all His majesty, resides. The place where no sun is needed because God

Himself is the source of light. The place that entirely erases the sting of death and strips it of victory.

If we could see the giant portrait of our existence in relation to the reality of heaven, perhaps surrender and submission to God's plan would be substantially easier. But maybe it is supposed to be hard-earned. Heaven is a REWARD. It's not a participation ribbon or a certification of satisfactory achievement; it is the compensation given to those who have entrusted their hearts to the God who authored every beat. Surrendering and submitting to God's eternal plan is worth it because the reward of heaven will be beyond our wildest imaginations. The return on such an investment far exceeds any possible comprehension.

Ashes to ashes, dust to dust, everything in this world will dwindle and end. Brilliant blooms will wither and fade. But our spirits? They are designed for heaven—that eternal home I cannot wrap my mind around yet spend countless hours attempting to imagine. Amy is there, and she sees it all. She is not "past-tense" but more alive than she has ever been. Likewise, our babies are held in God's hand, basking in His glorious presence. In light of all of this wonder, I begin to drop my questions and accusations to the ground once again. While I will always have complex feelings regarding Amy's passing, I am choosing daily to raise my arms in surrender and hand my life over in submission to the same God she worshiped in that hospital bed. One beautiful day, I will see her once again; and I am certain we will say our surrender was worth everything.

Oh death, where is your sting? You have no eternal victory for those who love the Lord.

you stopped breathing
the world kept turning
this is the most
incomprehensible injury
we must keep feeling

but it is here
in the wounding
our eyes are open
to the reality
of eternity

we are not
yet home

it seems unfair

even cruel

how we attempt to fit
an entire life
inside two paragraphs
of a newspaper
two hours of a service
one dash
between two dates
on a weathering stone
placed into the ground

life cannot be summarized
on such minuscule scales
for the details are too vast,
too important to exclude

if it were up to me
your fingerprints would be
etched into earth
as if to say,
"I was here
and every second mattered.

I felt it all
and every moment
will somehow be remembered."

so my heart will be this earth,
this sacred catalog of memory

just as softened dirt
allows feet to imprint
you are forever pressed into me
and as long as I am breathing
your details will be alive in memory

Chapter 28

A Gift

As someone who dreams wild, colorful, vivid dreams on a regular basis, I often wake up entirely fascinated. While my body rests, my mind is constantly at work weaving mysterious threads of thoughts and memory together. Sleeping, for me, usually means an instant teleportation into a lively world where basically anything is possible. I liken it to painting while both blindfolded and completely distracted—an involuntary array of colors are randomly scattered and blended onto a wide-open canvas.

While most of my dreams are like visiting abstract pieces of art in a museum, crinkling my nose as I try to make sense of the creations, there have been a handful of clear, concise, and meaningful dreams that have come as though they were gifts from God Himself.

On an early November morning, exactly one year after Amy's funeral, I was given one of these rare gifts. I had spent the entire year earnestly begging God to allow me to see even the tiniest glimpse of heaven. At times, anger fueled my request. But often, sorrow and curiosity intermingled into passionate conversation as I told God it simply was not fair

A Gift

Amy was there with Him while I was left here with only a hungry imagination.

What was she experiencing that I could only begin to paint a picture of? Every time I attempted to imagine heaven, I felt like an inadequate sketch artist given only a few clues to base my portrait upon. I wanted to know heaven as Amy knew it. I wanted to feel its textures, smell its scents, and walk arm-in-arm with Jesus as I matched my stride with His. Heaven seemed like a gathering I had not yet been invited to, and I was (and still am) entirely curious.

"God, what's it like? Please, give me even the smallest taste—even one drop—and I promise to stop endlessly begging," I said over and over in multiple ways over the course of a year, as if slamming fists on heaven's door, hoping to catch even a sliver through the smallest crack.

That morning in early November, I shot up in bed at exactly 6:30, startled awake from a dream. A gift. God had answered me in His own unique way. I can still close my eyes and recall the details so vividly.

In my dream, I was seated at a restaurant table enjoying time with our extended family. As everyone around me indulged in conversation, I picked up my brand-new cell phone and started scrolling through my contacts. Among the list of names, I found "Amy's cell phone" and tilted my head in curiosity. Amy didn't have a cell phone, and I wondered if I had added her by accident or had simply assigned her name to a wrong number.

After allowing curiosity to eat away at me for a few moments, I decided to call the mysterious number right there in the middle of the bustling restaurant. After a couple rings, a voice answered on the other end of the line. It was a voice so crisp, familiar, and astonishingly clear.

"Hello?"

"...Amy? Is this really YOU?" I asked, halfway choking on my own words.

"Yes, it's me!" she answered, her light voice wrapped in a giggle.

"But aren't you in heaven?"

"I am. Actually, I'm at a banquet feast right now!"

I could hear the sound of forks hitting plates, jovial laughter, and the hum of conversation floating through the phone line. It all seemingly melted together with the sounds of life from my own surroundings. She, too, was seated at a table, and just as the chatter of people enjoying each other's company encircled me, it also surrounded her.

"Okay, what? You're at a banquet? I have so many questions... hmmm. Okay, first of all, what's the food like?" I asked with a hunger for information heartier than my appetite for actual food.

"You wouldn't believe it if I described it to you. I don't even know how to describe it. But seriously, everything tastes *incredible*. There's nothing like it. You can eat as much as you want and never get full!"

At this, my mind started swirling with more questions.

"Ah! Really? I can't wait for that! Okay, so I need to know, if the food is that good, how is the music in heaven?" I have spent so many moments during times of worship squeezing my eyes tightly, trying to imagine the songs of heaven. A passage in Revelation often piques my curiosity and causes me to paint vivid images and sounds in my head, but I'm quite certain my imagination falls very short. Revelation 7:9-11 (NLT) reads:

> *"After this I saw a vast crowd, too great to count, from every nation and tribe and people and language, standing in front of the throne and before the Lamb. They were clothed in white robes and held palm branches in their hands. And they were shouting with a great*

roar, 'Salvation comes from our God who sits on the throne and from the Lamb!'"

While this passage doesn't explicitly say everyone was singing, as a musician I imagine the most glorious music accompanying this event. If I were there, I would most certainly be singing.

"Sarah, it's so true when 1 Corinthians 2:9 (NIV) says, *'What no eye has seen, no ear has heard, and no human heart has conceived —God has prepared the things for those who love him.'* There is NO WAY I can adequately describe to you just how amazing not only the music is here, but everything else, as well. You simply cannot know what heaven is like until you're here. I can honestly say there are no words complete enough to answer this question, along with others you might have."

Just as I was opening my mouth to plead my case to receive more answers, Amy cut into my thoughts with her enthusiasm and said, "Wait, there's someone here who wants to talk to you. Hold on..."

After listening to shuffling sounds, a voice came crisply through the phone line and said, "Hi, Sarah!"

I paused, eyes darting back and forth. This voice I had not heard since a month before my fourth birthday, yet in an instant I recognized him.

"UNCLE NORB?!" I exclaimed as my eyes began to well. "It's been so long. I miss you more than I can say!"

My uncle had passed away very suddenly from a hidden heart defect lurking in his body, and despite my young age at the time of his death, I hold very clear memories of him. I remember the times he would toss my cousins, sister, and me on his back while pretending to be a horse galloping across the living room; the time he won a blue stuffed bear at the fair and brought it home just for me; the moments he would play his guitar, singing worship songs to the Jesus he loved so dearly;

and the afternoons he would take us to the park to play with his new little puppy named Glory. Everything about him was memorable, even to a little child like myself.

I noticed Uncle Norb did not respond after I told him I missed him, nor did he acknowledge the time that had passed. Instead, he simply said, "I'm here enjoying heaven with my son."

Prior to his passing in early December of 1985, my uncle and his young wife learned they were expecting their first child. Just before he died, she tragically miscarried their precious baby five months along. At the time of this dream, I hadn't known their baby was a boy. After the fact, my mom and Oma both confirmed this to be true.

"Wow, your SON. Uncle Norb, I have to ask you a question I have always wondered. Are babies actually babies in heaven? I mean, are they infants you need to hold and care for?" It was a valid question, I thought.

"Eh, more or less. It's hard to describe," he said, leaving another question largely unanswered. "But hey, your Opa is here with me. Let me see if he would like to come to the phone to talk with you."

"Opa?! I would absolutely LOVE that!" I exclaimed.

After a brief moment, my uncle's voice came through the phone line once again. "He's too busy relaxing and enjoying everything to talk on the phone right now. He told me to tell you he'll see you later when you get here."

This was exactly my Opa's personality. While he was a hard worker, I have many memories of him sitting, laughing, relaxing, and enjoying our company over a good meal. He knew how to rest.

"Okay, I understand," I said. "But Uncle Norb, I miss you so much. It's hard to not be there with you. I can't wait to see you again."

"I'm very excited to see you, too, Sarah," he said with

tenderness in his familiar voice. "I should get back to the banquet right now, but we will talk again soon."

We said our "see-you-later's" and "I love you's" and hung up the phone. I looked across the table at my family members and tried to explain to them how I had just discovered a direct phone line to heaven. As I attempted to pluck words from an experience I couldn't quite explain, I startled out of my dream and everything paused abruptly like a TV show on commercial break.

Rubbing my eyes while trying to decipher dream from reality, I tiptoed out of bed to begin my day. As shower water hit my face, I began to smile, acknowledging God. "Okay, I see what You did. I suppose I have to keep my promise and quit bothering You about heaven."

I knew at that moment He had answered my prayer. He had given me the smallest glimpse of heaven without even utilizing my eyesight. While I knew I had not *really* spoken to my loved ones, He used this dream to teach me a few things about the eternity that awaits.

I didn't get to SEE anything. I did not get to learn about what it was like to share life with Jesus face to face or bask in the light of God's throne. I didn't witness the streets of gold or the pearly gates. However, even though I only had one question directly answered (praise God there will be amazing food paired with open appetites in heaven), I learned there is so much life and so much enjoyment ahead. Food, music, relaxation, and community will still be a part of us but in a wildly improved form. Here on earth, Amy did not have a chance to meet my Uncle Norb, yet in heaven they were sharing a meal together.

Just imagine all the connections we will have instant access to. We will be able to enjoy eternity with those who entered heaven thousands of years before us and with people who will come after. Alongside our loved ones and those we never had the pleasure of knowing on earth, we will enjoy laughter, conversation, meals, and worship. Our individual stories will melt together as we spend eternity together in the fullness of God.

This would suggest death is truly a doorway to a richer, more robust life. It is not the end of the story but instead an awakening to completion. We will be with God, together, in perfection for all of eternity.

While I am not attempting to tuck this dream given to me into the pages of Scripture, it is a gift I cannot keep to myself. It was given to me so I can share this with you. There is so very much ahead—unimaginable fullness of life, as Scripture promises, for those who believe in Him. As the familiar passage states in John 3:16 (NIV), *"For God so loved the world that he gave his one and only Son, that whoever believes in him shall not perish but have eternal life."*

Not only will we live eternally in the paradise of heaven *with* God, but the trials, pain, and heartache of this earthly life will forever be concepts of the past. While I told both Amy and Uncle Norb I missed them, neither returned such words to me. Quite simply, they did not miss me because they knew I would be with them one day. For them, time is not an issue and waiting is but a bat of the eyelash. They are too caught up in the wonder of heaven and aren't afforded space in their minds to miss what was no longer in front of them. I am reminded of the Scripture in 2 Corinthians 4:17 (NIV) that says, *"For our light and momentary troubles are achieving for us an eternal glory that far outweighs them all."* Though we are often swallowed by the troubles of this life, the beauty of an eternity found in heaven outweighs all of it. Every trial and each struggle is entirely temporary. And while the temporary overwhelms, the eternal liberates.

Ever since experiencing this dream, I truly have not begged God for further detail. I cannot begin to know the beautiful

A Gift

details of heaven until I arrive. No, my appetite for the unknown eternity has not waned, but the certainty of eternal hope keeps me focused in the face of temporary trials. Yes, it's so important to "live for today," but it is more important to live with eternity in mind. One day I will live in this fantastic place where the word "goodbye" will entirely cease. Death is a final parting wave to this earth as we know it. It is also a beautiful first "hello" to an eternity void of worry, sickness, tears, fear, and loss of every kind. For the Christ follower, death is an awakening into new life abundant with unimaginable riches. The promise of heaven and an eternity with our amazing Creator turns surrender into the richest of treasure. This strips death of its seemingly terrifying sting.

Everything will pass through our hands here on earth, but oh, what fullness we will have for the keeping in heaven. I will have an armload of children to hold while living in God's direct presence *forever*. I will know their names. I will memorize their faces and the flecks of color in their eyes. I will see and experience goodness on an entirely new level. I will see Jesus' face while feeling His palm in mine. What color are HIS eyes? What does His audible voice sound like? What new name has He given to me? What does the Father's throne look like? What hue is the sky? Wait, what if there's not even a sky, but some unknown canopy immeasurably more wonderful? I will know all these details, and so much more.

Pause for a moment and think about what awaits you. Can you even begin to wrap your mind around it? Can your imagination begin to give shapes, colors, feelings, and understanding to eternity? Not yet, of course, but what hope we have! All these endings we have faced will be redeemed beyond our wildest dreams.

enfold me in Your truths
and strengthen me
with long-range vision
so I am not easily
enslaved by
temporary feelings

will it hurt?

every single day

but it will all be
as vapor
when I step into
eternity

Chapter 29

Fear and Anxiety

It was sometime after two o'clock in the morning, and I awoke with a startle. No, it was not a lovely dream about heaven, nor was it a vivid dream about drowning that separated me from sleep in an instant. In fact, it was not a dream at all. It was the presence of fear.

I sat up in bed and felt as though a hand cupped across my mouth to steal the air from my lungs. Kirk began stirring in his sleep next to me and I could hear Addie moving around in her bed from across the hall. It was as if fear had broken into our home, floated down the corridors, and crept under our covers with uninvited, sticky fingers. I felt choked by its darkness and accompanying anxiety. The atmosphere felt unsettled, and my heartbeat quickened in response.

Although I did not hear an audible voice, various venomous sentences bled into my mind. "You're sick. The process is going to be horrible. You're going to be absolutely miserable. You're dying. You won't be here to see Addie grow up." The thoughts went on for some time, and I felt so many layers of anxiety and panic descend all in one swoop. I listened.

I bought into the voice and paid close attention. Various worst-case scenarios began playing like a movie reel in my mind.

You see, I had been experiencing problematic health symptoms and my doctor had found cause for investigation. The following day would hold a series of medical tests to see if anything was amiss in my body, so naturally I was concerned. I knew absolutely nothing about what was ahead, but fear and anxiety barged through the door like uninvited guests speaking rousing phrases to my concern. In those early morning hours, I entertained such trespassers. It was as though I told them, "Oh, you've broken into our home? That's quite alright. Here, sit at my table while I put on some tea and serve you some cherry pie. I want to hear all you have to say. Stay a while."

Out of everything I have surrendered in my life, whether voluntarily or involuntarily, these two things have been the most difficult to hand over to God: fear and anxiety. Even though the Lord has been so patient with me, and despite all the incredibly deep lessons He has allowed me to learn, this "dynamic duo" creeps in like a disease time and time again. Just as moonflowers are susceptible to various kinds of mold and disease, fear and anxiety are the sicknesses that so easily take over root, vine, and bloom in my own life. They have stunted so much growth, and I have often allowed it. Quite honestly, I have held a defensive hand up against God and said, "No. I don't trust You with all of this. I'd rather entertain the rot of anxiety than confront the gross amount of unbelief I have in my life."

Is it not disobedient disbelief from which "unhealthy" fear and anxiety stem? By adopting these thought patterns as truth, I do not believe God is who He says He is. I say He will leave me and forsake me. I assume He does not work all things together for my good. I fear the worst found in the temporary instead of locking eyes with the eternal. I allow the anxiety coiling around my worst fears permission to choke out joy and trust.

Hear me: While *feeling* fear and anxiety is not a sin,

welcoming them—inviting them to stay, indulging upon their venomous agendas, and in turn feeding them more attention—is incredibly unhealthy. Saying, "This is just something I deal with. It's just a part of who I am," is a lazy cop-out from actually staring disbelief in the face and addressing it. I recognize this. And while I know many deal with chemical imbalances and medical reasons for anxiety, I do know this is not the home in which I am designed to set up permanent residence. I firmly believe NONE of us are created to adopt the labels fear and anxiety are eager to slap on us.

No, this is not the place in which we are designed to live. Fear and anxiety are like shabby, disgusting jail cells that hold us hostage when we could be reclining in beautiful, jewel-adorned palaces. Oh, how often we insist upon rot instead of health. And if we are honest, we are often very willing hostages. Quite honestly, it is easier to fear than to trust. It is less challenging to worry than it is to have faith. It is more convenient to doubt than it is to believe. And especially, when we have been let down, hurt, discouraged, or have experienced the worst of the worst, we have a great arsenal of excuses to allow our unbelief to spiral. We feel entitled to stay planted in our fears and anxieties because we are familiar with nightmares coming true. And in this state, our ears hear the voice of the enemy quicker than the voice of the Father. As my dear friend Ben has wondered, "Why do we listen to the voice of the enemy? He doesn't love us." Good question.

I personally have been wounded; therefore, I have seemingly involuntary, protective responses. I can *speak* of surrender and submission, but the aftereffects of my losses are very real and frequently feed my disbelief. I can easily raise my hands in an act of surrender to God, but less often my heart does the same. There is often a disconnect between what I say I believe and what my heart of hearts believes to be true. When it comes down to it, I am fearful and anxious because I simply do not trust God. I, once again, desire control. I easily believe my worrisome thoughts and actions can actually obtain such a thing. Open-handed living slips to the wayside, and once again I tighten my grip. I have experienced worst-case scenarios, and even though God has graciously walked beside me through it all, I often cling to fear instead of Him. I listen to the enemy who hates me more than I tune my ear to the voice of the One who deeply loves me. How insanely ludicrous.

However, I am challenged when I think back to that lovely walk I had with God on that gorgeous summer evening. Remember the one in which I felt His presence surround me like a cloak that felt like a song of deliverance? If I decide to wear God's presence as a garment, this means I will face every situation in life with Him. I will never be alone. Everything that comes my way must first go through Him, my covering, the One who delivers me from that which hinders with even a song. If I truly believe He is my armor (Ephesians 6:10-18), then His presence is my protection in every situation. Yes, I will be able to feel the presence of fear and anxiety, but only when I allow unbelief to form a crack in the cloak of His covering will I be wholly consumed by them.

Am I saying the fear and anxiety I have wrestled with my entire life is my fault alone? Absolutely not. There is a very real enemy who uses these tactics on ALL of us. He's not creative; he is incredibly predictable. According to the National Alliance on Mental Illness, anxiety disorders are the most common mental health concern in the United States. Over forty million adults in the United States have a documented anxiety disorder.[1] This is nearly twenty percent of the population of our country. And this number doesn't even reflect those who have not sought professional help. How staggering.

It is likely safe to say ALL of us feel the effects of fear and anxiety, and we cannot help when they bust through the doors of our homes and begin ransacking our peace. We are the ones, however, who pull up chairs and invite them to stay instead of demanding their departure. That part is on us. Our disbelief in God's goodness, sovereignty, and ability to care for us in every circumstance is what we all need to daringly stare in the eyes and dissect. We need to seriously evaluate what we are hosting in our lives.

Yes, it is healthy to seek therapy from professionals; and yes, there is a place for medication. I have done both. However, statistics and personal experiences tell us anxiety is rampant despite. Without also challenging our disbelief in God, there will always be a missing piece. We must dig into ourselves to investigate and uncover such roots, but we cannot mend this sickness on our own.

All throughout summer and fall, moonflowers can be subject to various diseases, but the flower itself does not have the power to rid itself of such things. The gardener must help the roots, vines, and blooms when botanical illnesses appear. Likewise, we cannot completely declare victory over the toxicity of fear and anxiety in our own striving alone. Our Great Gardener has all the tools necessary to help us find healing in this area of our lives. He is not intimidated (nor is He scared away) by our feelings and unbelief. He longs to examine us as we willingly and honestly unfold our complicated layers before Him. He alone holds the remedy in His healing presence. His Word is the healing salve to every disease, and nothing is too complicated for His wise counsel.

When it comes to my own anxiety, I am constantly a work in progress. I have come to a place where I refuse to accept fear and anxiety as my "normal" or use it as a part of my definition. Second Peter 2:19 (NIV) says, *"People are slaves to whatever has mastered them."* I do not want to be fear's captive. I do not desire to wear the shackles of anxiety. I do not wish to bow before them as their defeated slave.

Those early morning hours when my attention was caught

up in their cunning lies, I realized my need for the truth. I recognized deceit. I cut my whisper through the darkness and called them out by name, demanding they leave. "Spirit of fear, spirit of anxiety, get out of here in Jesus' name. You're not from God. You're not welcome here. LEAVE." Shortly thereafter, I fell back asleep, and the next thing I recall, I was opening my eyes to fresh morning sunlight slicing through the blinds. The new day ahead would reveal all my medical testing as benign; and while surgery would be needed in my future, there was no life-threatening disease to be found in the immediate present. The fear and anxiety I entertained turned out to waste precious time and rest.

Even if my results had come back differently, unhealthy fear and anxiety would have played no helpful roles. None. They are completely useless when it comes to helping me through anything. In fact, enslaving myself to their endless whims is often so much worse than experiencing that which I fear the most. Therefore, the real question I ask myself is this: how much fear and anxiety will I choose to hold on to, or will I decide to surrender it all to God and His gentle, healing expertise? I cannot trust God and continue to carry anxiety. I cannot hope in Him and fear. Like oil and water, these things do not mix. If my hands are locked in His and my heart is filled with His nearness, there is no room for disease of the soul. His promises are far too abundant for such dualism.

While it is not in my ability to stand up to fear and anxiety in my own strength, it is up to me to honestly bring my unbelief before God and allow Him to repair the cracks in the cloak of His covering. He is rightly able to do so when I am brutally honest, humbly obedient, and bravely willing with open hands. To obtain the health I desire, I must surrender fear and anxiety every time they barge through the door to disrupt my peace. I am not their servant; I am God's. My Master does not speak anxious thoughts and fearful feelings into my life; demons do.

Who will I permit as Lord over my life? I cannot serve two masters, this I know.

I was not created to live in fear and anxiety, and the same is true for you. While we will all continue to feel the effects of unhealthy fear and anxiety here on earth, surrendering such things repeatedly is the key to unlocking the handcuffs they toss around our wrists. Instead of fear and anxiety enslaving us, we are to take THEM captive in submission to God.

We could never "arrive" at a perfect level of mastery over fear and anxiety in our own strength, but we can serve the One who is already master over them. He is the only one who can heal such rot so we can live life to the full, no matter the situations we walk through. As long as we entertain fear and anxiety, they will continue to reveal areas in our lives where we are lacking and expose holes dug by unbelief. May we now begin to uncover them instead of making homes in their wastelands so we can be filled with the peace of His presence instead.

potential endings
dreaded outcomes
collect into piles
of rot

anxiety

the name etched above
this graveyard of soot and ash
where countless moments
have been put to death

"but which is worse?" I ask myself

living endless days of dread
unwrapping one fear
only to find it wears three heads
throwing days
YEARS
into their gaping mouths

or actually experiencing
that which is awful
and realizing

I am not only surviving
but given the option
of overcoming

Chapter 30

Let Go

I will not blame God for the tragedies I have faced. I will only blame the fallen state of our temporary, sin-swept world.
I open my hands and let go.

I hate what I have gone through, but I am thankful God's strength was displayed in my weakest moments.
I open my hands and let go.

I will not fear what the future brings, for I have weathered many situations and I am still here blooming. Whatever joys and trials lie ahead, I am hidden under God's covering and I am not alone.
I open my hands and let go.

I will not be anxious for that which I cannot control. I will not waste my precious time and energy on cyclical, pointless worry. Such things serve no purpose if I am to grow.
I open my hands and let go.

I will not hold on to anger toward others nor hold resentment toward God. Instead, I will point holy rage toward the enemy of our souls while refusing to give him even the smallest foothold on my soul.

I open my hands and let go.

I will recognize there is so much goodness found in this imperfect life. Even in the worst situations, I will see there are so many opportunities to deepen my faith while discovering what truly satisfies.

I open my hands and let go.

I will not wither in night seasons sure to come. I will dig my roots deeper into the soil in which I am placed. I will tilt my head to the night sky and count all the shining blessings twinkling in the darkness.

I open my hands and let go.

I am seen, known, and deeply loved by the Creator of my soul. Even when I feel like a forgotten failure in my disbelief and disobedient wandering, His adoring gaze is still fixed on me. When I feel worthless, He calls me worthy of His affections, forgiveness, grace, and tender direction. When I grieve, He is near.

He is mine, and I am His. To Him alone will I hold.

what would happen
if you opened up your chest
and released all those demons
you have held under self-arrest?

what if you named them one by one
and yelled, "I RELEASE YOU!"
with all the strength in your lungs?

they would scatter
swallowed by the wind
and you would finally be free
to flourish as who
you were created to be

Chapter 31

Dancing in October

I have a difficult time selecting a favorite season, as there are characteristics found in all four that capture my attention. Where I reside, however, there is something entirely special about the month of October. In seemingly the tiniest wink, mature green gives way to wild, otherworldly hues. Colors become so rich, they overwhelm in a generous buffet for the senses. Branches become sleeved in honeyed marigold, fiery orange, ruby red, and velvet burgundy. I like to imagine that the trees have dressed in their finest ball gowns overnight, and losing track of time, are found waltzing about in the early morning light still donned in their finest. As for the sun, it hangs lower and kinder in the sky, draping an amber veil upon everything it touches. Dried grass crisps underfoot, apple cider stews on the stove, and last bits of the garden are picked and tilled. Autumn is a gentle process of letting go of all that grew and flourished under the summer sky. Autumn is the most beautiful surrender.

On a slow October afternoon, I pushed open the screen door and padded down the pavement. The sky above was cornflower blue, the air unseasonably warm, and the trees adorned in most luxurious hues. What a perfect moment to steal away from to-do lists and expectations to enjoy a long walk.

As I made my way down our country road, I reached a certain point where the trees canopied over pavement like a golden trellis. With not a passing car in sight, I stopped on the side of the road, lifted my head to the sky, and observed. Leaves untethered from branches and floated softly to the ground one after another, and it was as though I was observing nature itself softly letting go. It was not a grand affair shouting out for attention; it was a simple, natural response to the shifting season. Nothing can stay. Nature itself knows this fully well. In my noticing, I wondered if I could let go, too.

I closed my eyes and began speaking to God. I unfurled a whole collection of cares laying deep inside my heart, laying them bare before Him under those lemon-tinted leaves. I seem to be very good at doing this over and over again. As I emptied my familiar ache born of loss, I once again became filled with a gentle sense of peace. His presence was there with me among the crisped, falling leaves and the surrender of my heart. By seeking Him again, I was repairing all those cracks I had allowed to form in His covering. Allowing Him to carry my burdens frees my heart and hands for the lightness of holding His presence.

I began responding to God's undeniable gentleness in the most undignified manner: I began to worship on the side of our quiet country road. Lifting my arms, I began singing my own song to the only One who is truly able to make my heart light. Unabashedly, I began to dance. Cascading leaves brushed past my face as I twirled about. Even if someone else had been around, I would not have cared. I felt so light and so very free, and it didn't matter if I appeared to be a lunatic. Appearances, after all, do not matter one bit. My song and my dance were simply a response of surrender to my King. I was entirely enjoying Him, and He was enjoying me. Intimacy.

When it comes to surrendering to God, I am often hesitant because of control and unmerited distrust. However, when I sacrifice all things—difficult, ugly, wonderful, and good—in order to know Him more, they are replaced with experiences far more beautiful than I could have imagined. And when I submit difficult feelings and situations before Him, He gives strength and wisdom beyond my own power. No matter what angle I view surrender to God in, it is always the wisest thing I can do.

Instead of simply wishing my hardships away, I am now realizing the opportunities to experience His patient, abiding grace and His stunning, capable strength hidden inside each one. Just as I did on that autumn afternoon, I worship God time and time again by surrendering that which constantly tries to keep my hands filled with tasks, my mind filled with anxiety, and my heart filled with anger and fear. The lightness of His presence is worth every bit of sacrifice.

There are lessons hidden in blazing autumn leaves, after all. Yes, vibrant summer greens are full of life, but there's something particularly wonderful about the way they glow while letting go. In the face of death, something inside of them seems to unhinge. It is as though their colors sing, "Don't hold back, hold on, or live so reservedly. Live right now! It's all or nothing! Look how you can shine! Look how beautiful it is to surrender!" The leaves are arguably the most beautifully alive when they are in a season of letting go. Could the same be true for us?

Rest cannot come until surrender is practiced. In fact, the road of surrender and submission may appear differently for all of us. Some are winding while others include hills and valleys. Still others are short and straightforward while some include a variation of seemingly everything. But no matter the journey, surrender and submission lead to the same destination: the beautifully vibrant peace of His everlasting, abiding presence. And oh, what a freeing place that is to be.

apple trees
domes of green
cast shadows
of lush Persian rugs
across soft lawn

I lie in the shade
running fingertips atop
slivers of green
listening to ripened fruit
thump against the ground
in heaps

a collection of sweet
wasted
so it seems

I cannot gather the abundance
in my arms
I cannot taste all their goodness
upon my tongue

but I pick up just one
biting past crisp red

wiping juice
with the back of my hand
I have tasted what I could and that is enough

Chapter 32

Rest is Surely Coming

After snapping our moonflower pods off the vine in late autumn, I held a few in the palm of my hand. I knew just past the exterior lay little chambers of seed that could be broken, soaked, planted, and brought to a place of flourishing under the starry sky. So much potential. It is difficult to imagine how minuscule seeds hold beautiful worlds of possibility in their bellies, but with proper tending, they will one day bloom, too.

I noticed old, fallen blossoms wilted on top of the soil—last summer's beauty returning to dirt. Yes, this was sad, but so very natural. Gardeners do not grow vegetables without the end goal of harvest. Flowers are not grown with the expectation of eternal bloom void of seasons of rest. Those moonflower seedpods in my palm reminded me that autumn is not merely a season of death but a time of preparing for what is ahead. The old must be surrendered in order to enjoy rest. And both surrender and rest are necessary to bloom once again.

I gathered the moonflower pods and brought them inside. I pruned the vines and raked the soil. After all, the first frost of

Rest is Surely Coming

the approaching winter had already blanketed the ground. Now it was time to prepare for a season of rest.

trust
is not the absence
of discomfort
but the faith
I will never be alone
through every hill and valley
of this mapless journey

Part Four
Rest

bare branches stretch a thousand fingers to a muted sky
swaying back and forth as the wind brushes by

it sounds like an echo of a tune hummed in August
when trees don themselves in the finest emerald dresses

but here in the darkness after surrendering their colors
and releasing beauty embellished in the belly of summer

they waltz to a refrain held as memory
and whisper a secret revealing mystery

as I close my eyes and listen in the deep winter blue
I hear them singing, "is this not so very beautiful, too?"

Chapter 33

Joy Remains

Daylight shrinks as the star-laden sky stretches out for a longer stay and a hush of winter tide settles over the land. Bare tree branches slip icy veils over their outstretched arms and the summer hum of chattering insects and bellowing frogs gives way to simple whispers of wind swishing through towering pines. Falling snowflakes gather into lacy-white heaps on the ground and rivers begin to slow. Sandals are exchanged for clunky boots and swimsuits for wooly-soft hats and mittens. The frosty season of cold has officially arrived.

Admittedly, I used to deeply despise winter. In our corner of the world, the chilly months seem to take their time passing by. Days are largely spent indoors as the frigid outside air pricks like needles against skin, and at times it is difficult to enjoy this season whose landscape is simplified and void of a vast assortment of color. It is icy, dark, and muted. While many people prefer the cold months, it has taken me a bit of time to realize the goodness hidden inside its frozen grip. When my family and I moved from the city into our little country home, I began to realize there might be more to winter than simply shivering and complaining. There had to be more. I was tired of spending half of every year grumbling the days away while hiding indoors. What a waste.

I knew it was up to me to learn how winter could be a season of much joy. Joy, after all, is a choice and I had to discover it for myself. Over time, I began to realize that with the right set of eyes and the proper frame of mind, it could be found hidden in plain sight.

On a January evening, Kirk, Addie, and I grabbed our ice skates, walked out into the woods, and headed toward the newly frozen pond tucked under a collection of spindly trees. Since our previous residence in the city did not afford too many opportunities to skate, our first laps around the pond were filled with giggles, clumsy flails, and wobbly ankles. Even after gaining a bit of confidence on the ice, the occasional dramatic fall promised its presence among our gliding. And oh my, how we laughed! While Kirk quickly regained his old hockey moves from his youth, Addie and I felt like baby giraffes learning how to use our legs for the very first time.

Seemingly on cue, and as though we were in a Hallmark movie, soft snowflakes began to fall. I tilted my face upward, opened my mouth, and caught a few on my tongue. I stood still on the surface of the pond and widened my arms, trying to collect as many flakes as I could on my coat. This was something I didn't get to experience every day, so I thought perhaps I should embrace it for a while. It felt like joy. It felt like rest. Right in the middle of a season I was so used to disliking, I thought maybe my mind could be changed. Surely winter months were not created to simply be despised. They were not designed to be some sort of torture chamber of cruel and unusual punishment. I knew there was a deeper purpose I had not yet fully allowed myself to experience. More than occasional ice-skating sessions and catching snowflakes on my tongue, what other delicacies did winter hold that I had not yet realized? Right there, with ice skates on my feet and snowflakes on my arms, I breathed a silent prayer asking God to show me how to enjoy a season I dread each year.

My prayer began to unfold an answer right in front of me on that layer of ice, for that night I found joy had the power to thaw away layers of my self-imposed crabbiness. Simple joy opened my eyes wider to beautiful experiences sitting right under my nose. Under a graphite sky speckled with falling snow, an important shift took place inside of me as I took a little step forward in not wasting what was meant for embracing. It led to further wonderings of how I could begin to decide to enjoy something I previously grumbled about.

On the surface of that glassy pond, I opened my arms wider to the snow and kept skating until my ankles simply couldn't handle any more. The three of us walked back to our home and snuggled under blankets, our cheeks and noses glowing rosy-pink as they warmed. I felt joy multiplying where it had been accustomed to staying frozen solid, and I was certain it was not meant to stay in the boundaries of that moment. It was meant to thaw and recklessly spill all over the place. Not every winter day includes skating across ice under falling snow, but each one does include an invitation to appreciate and enjoy instead of despise. Each day asks to be lived, not merely survived. I am no longer interested in hating the days I am given because of the surrounding weather or varying circumstances. Joy does not have to come and go; it can steadily remain despite the season's change.

step out gently
into the dazzling early darkness
and breathe in deeply
of crisp, violet sky
whose stars wrap gently
around a glowing, opal moon
and bow lowly
as if to rest
in the freshly gathered field

watch bonfire embers
float as tiny orange feathers
bright and quiet
into deep onyx

smile knowing
there is nothing exceedingly dreadful
nothing terribly awful
in a cold winter's evening

(you will despise
only what you choose
to despise)

Chapter 34

Abide

If moonflowers could speak, we likely wouldn't hear their voices as they sit in their little-seeded state in the winter. We would only hear tiny, soft snores coming from their rounded bellies. As it is for most vegetation in climates subject to cold temperatures, winter simply means "rest." Those new moonflower seeds do not labor, toil, complain, or strive to accomplish—they simply *are*. They lie and wait. Germination and bloom are saved for another day; but for now, winter bids them to be still.

As we know, plants and trees are still very much alive and ticking in cold months, but they also sit dormant and cease production for a season. This dormancy, this rest, is not only an example of their God-given housekeeping skills but is also necessary to their survival. In this pause, proteins are broken down and remade, cell membranes are maintained, and metabolism is slowed. Winter offers moments of rejuvenating sleep before vegetation is asked to expel energy in milder weather once again. Before and after they DO, they rest. This is a very important part of their life cycle.

Marni, a wonderful friend of mine, frequently recites a phrase that catches my attention. She says, "We are human BE-ings before we are human DO-ings." How often I tend to forget this while living an abundant life teeming with a constant hum of activity. Like most people, I feel like a slave to never-ending to-do lists. Each new day brings about a new collection of tasks to accomplish, people to see, problems to tackle, provision to find, and success to achieve. I am often caught in the current that tells me I need to have a successful career while cultivating a healthy family, a vibrant social life, and a clean home all while helping to meet the needs of others around me. Simultaneously, I am supposed to maintain my own physical and mental health while continuing in my own journey of healing. And what about my spiritual life? Where is time afforded to properly attend to that?

Can long-term spiritual health (let alone any other type of flourishing) be tended to while keeping the hurried pace I set for myself in attempt to fill expectations our society has led me to believe are required? I don't think so—not if I believe the things I do and accomplish are what defines me first and foremost. If I am ever weary in life, it is not necessarily my surrounding circumstances that have sucked my strength dry but my lack of resting and abiding with Christ. My weariness is in direct relation to where He falls in order of importance in my life.

But here is a beautiful truth: God is not a task to accomplish but an oasis of rest. He does not belong on my to-do lists because time with Him should never be a completed chore to check off. Time with Him is meant to be savored and never-ending, not rushed and expiring. After all, our relationship with God should be full of participating and engaging instead of meeting goals found at the end of checklists. Realizing and experiencing His presence puts goal-seeking to shame, for His presence is not something to achieve but a reality to enjoy.

Revisiting John 15:4-5, the English Standard Version of the Bible uses the word "abide" instead of "remain." It reads, *"**Abide** in me, and I in you. As the branch cannot bear fruit by itself, unless it **abides** in the vine, neither can you, unless you **abide** in me. I am the vine; you are the branches. Whoever **abides** in me and I in him, he bears much fruit, for apart from me you can do nothing"* (emphasis added). While this word has multiple definitions, the biblical meaning is to stay. Yes, I can stay next to Jesus' side amidst all the busy tasks in my life as though I am a mere passenger along for the ride, but reading these verses causes me to desire a certain stillness I easily lack. Perhaps He would love for me to defy the rushed pace of daily life in order to make space to rest with Him before I do all the other things. While I cannot change a lot of the demands naturally placed upon me, when I abide with Jesus, things do change because I no longer bear anything alone.

If I really scrutinize my schedule, I see how much time I truly waste on things that don't matter much at all. I think about the time I have spent scrolling and admiring little boxes representing the best of people's lives online. I consider the television series I have binged and all the movies I have watched. I am reminded of the entertainment I have consumed and the time I have wasted on things that pass as quickly as the wind. While nothing is particularly wrong with these things, I say I am busy when I have plenty of space to tend to this precious relationship I have with God. I have filled my mind with lesser entertainment instead of hushing the noise to rest with Him.

Like those little moonflower seeds, rest is entirely necessary for human health and well-being. Physical sleep is paramount to our bodies, as God hardwired this need into us. It makes sense, then, that we are also made to take pauses in other areas of our lives. Just as a good night's rest affords wellness to our bodies, resting and abiding *with* Christ seems to accelerate mental and spiritual health. It is here we become still enough to reorient ourselves with the One who created us while intimately spending time with the only Source who gives lasting strength. When we are with Him, we discover who we truly are because our ears are emptied of other noise. He is the only one who can tell us who we are, as lesser identities bow to His definitions. While abiding with Him, all that is unhealthy and damaged is broken down to be remade into something new. We are slowed enough for God to do important maintenance in our lives. Resting and abiding, therefore, are holy practices. It is in this beautifully slow time we find medicine for our wounded souls.

A couple years ago, I was introduced to the concept of spiritual direction at just the right time in my life. I was only considering authoring this book, and I was truly seeking furthered healing from our five miscarriages. However, I had become incredibly busy doing all the life things instead of simply being. I was caught in a cycle of striving and not often abiding. I was trying to schedule time with God, and by the end of each day, I usually beat myself up for missing the mark. My life was too loud to hear what He wanted to say. I was too busy with lesser things to truly abide with God. I expected myself to maintain an impossible standard of always creating, achieving, and hustling instead of practicing times of rest.

In spiritual direction, one is encouraged to slow down enough to perceive the ways God is already moving amidst life's moments and situations. It is stilling ears, hushing noise, and pausing demanding schedules. It is putting away various forms of media and valuing silence. It is submitting one's hurry to God in order to discover slower, healthier patterns. It is unlocking the colorful imagination so many have stifled since childhood to allow for God to speak life into weary gray.

Bev, my spiritual director, has patiently helped me carve away the unnecessary in order to create more meaningful time spent with God. The spiritual exercises she leads me through demonstrate just how holy the still and ordinary can be. As it turns out, the quiet moments can bubble and teem with new life. While Bev does not counsel or tell me what to do, she leads me through slowed prayer and imaginative exercises that truly help me better see the ways God is constantly at work in my circumstances. She has shown me how to incorporate holding silence among the blaring noise of life. Through a couple years of guidance, I have learned ways to feel the calm of His presence even on my craziest, most abundantly scheduled days. I have better understood how to abide with Christ through all the moments of my days and layers of grief.

These habits of holy rest have accelerated my healing. While yes, I will continue to mournfully ache because of my temporary losses, abiding with Christ has shown me that my permanent home is not found in pain's dingy structures. Time with Him has allowed me to slow down enough to address the parts of me that I have been too busy to heal. It has been much like sweeping and dusting an old, forgotten attic space to allow for decluttering and renovation. I am clearing out the haze in order to create a restful space to return to again and again. I'm revisiting old depressive patterns less and less as I wrap myself in who He says I am. And while abiding, what have I heard Him say? More than I could ever express. I could fill page after page and book after book with etchings from His voice, but what stands out as a beacon of beautifully illuminated hope is this: He has given me my definition.

"Sarah, you are worthy of My love. You are Mine. You don't have to strive. If you never wear another definition in this life besides being My child, that is enough. You are seen by My eyes, and you do not have to hide. You are not a target of continual loss and you have access to the healing salve constantly flowing from My hands. It is for you. *I Am* for you."

When such simple, profound words are pressed into my

heart from the Creator and Sustainer of the universe, true beauty begins to emerge. How, then, could I not make space to abide with Him? Time spent with Him is advantageous to my health and well-being. Abiding with Him does not allow me to stay the same but gives me hope and strength necessary for a lasting, flourishing future. It is here I am both defined and refined.

Taking time to be still in His presence is a practice of becoming like Christ. Just think of all the times in the Gospels He retreated from the crowds in order to spend time with the Father. He never said, "Hey, everyone, pause your responsibilities, go grab a cup of coffee, and meet with Me in a quiet place regularly," but He constantly demonstrated the importance of rest through the way He lived. I imagine His ministry may have swallowed Him whole without such times spent abiding with the Father.

None of us live above the need for patterns of rest and silence in our lives. None of us can find health in non-stop rush. Instead, Jesus' life teaches us this: if the Maker of the universe rested and spent time abiding with the Father, so should we. There will always be excuses and opportunities to fill every second of our days with lesser things, but we will never escape the inherent need to abide with the One who sustains us in every way.

Take a moment right now, reader. Set down this book, as it is far inferior from the Word of God. Quiet phone notifications, log off social media, hire a babysitter if need be, and take whatever means necessary to find a quiet spot. Pause, breathe, and meet with God. Feast on His Word. Enjoy His creation. Simply BE—and not just once, but on repeat. You are only too busy because you have allowed it.

God is right next to you amidst the crazy days, but sometimes we need to change things up to better recognize Him. Yes, our brain might continue to rush and hum with chatter, but allow Him to meet you in such a state. Abiding is a *practice*, after all. Sometimes practice is messy, but it always perfects. Let God lovingly, gently perfect your soul through simplicity. He's waiting for you.

what if stillness
is rebellion against
every pace
the world attempts
to set for you

may the bowing of my heart
be as the breathing of my lungs

immediate
innate

and necessary
for my flourishing

Chapter 35

This is Worship, Too

Several months ago, a giant storm whipped through our corner of the world and the accompanying straight-line winds produced a heap of devastating damage. By the time angry clouds rolled away, many of the towering trees I had come to know on my countryside walks were laying on the ground in heaps and mangled ruins. I never realized mourning the loss of trees is a real thing until I had come to know, love, and appreciate them for myself. I had learned the personalities of individual trees. I knew how and when they budded and shed, the ways in which they danced and clapped in the wind, and the cuts and blemishes etched into their rough skin, among so many other things. I even ran my hands across some of their trunks and wondered what stories they held within their rings. Feeling the trees was like running fingertips across oaken braille. What had the trees silently witnessed throughout the years? What tales could they tell? But now, many of the trees I loved were destroyed.

Several of the trees across our river snapped and fell, and one plunged partially into the riverbank, dunking long, spindly fingers into the current. Partially attached to a still-rooted trunk, it remains to this day bobbing up and down in the passing water. The tree lost its life, but it continues to make a lovely sound.

Through listening to the sound of wooden resistance in the water, I made an observation: if there were no downed trees sitting in our backyard river, the water would be considerably quieter. We would not be able to hear gentle movement obediently wisping downstream if there were no disruptions in the current's path. As sad as it is to have lost that tree across our river, it pairs with passing river water to make a beautiful sound of current bubbling against branches. The disruption of a storm brought about a certain character. It is as though the tragedy of months past is still humming a song. I hear it while walking along the edges of our backyard, sitting on the porch reading a book, gathering around a crackling backyard bonfire, and even from inside as it floats through the open windows. In fact, the song is even heard as the river grows icy and slow with winter's approach. Swells of ice push and pop against the tree and the old tune of grief plays like a melody.

Yesterday's tragedies can sing. Is this not a form of worship?

Recently, my husband delivered a sermon to our congregation talking about how we often get stuck in unhealthy, cyclical patterns of reaction. The premise was this: a difficult circumstance or situation triggers us and we, in turn, try to solve issues on our own or go to everyone else to talk about it. We might avoid the feelings associated with it or point the finger to cast blame. Some of these options lead to stagnation while others give us a false sense of victory, but none lead to lasting health. And when the next trigger occurs, we find ourselves in the same cycle with nothing truly solved in a wise manner.

However, a choice can be made when difficult situations, challenging circumstances, or terrible tragedies trigger. We don't have to stay in the old patterns that have failed to lead us to lasting victory. Instead, we can CHOOSE to worship. We can sing amidst tragedy. We can even sing louder in the face of great grief. While other possible choices are knee-jerk responses, worship takes effort. But it is always a choice. I think of what my friend Pastor Tom has said: "The quality of our circumstance does not dictate God's worthiness of our worship." Yes, indeed.

When difficulty comes, there is always an invitation and opportunity to take time to worship before anything else happens—even if it means worshiping while swallowed whole by all the sticky feelings. Even if it means worshiping when it would be easier and more desirable to do something else. Even if it means worshiping while in the fire of grief. Even if it means worshiping when the whole world yells, "THAT doesn't make sense!"

When we worship, we set ourselves up for receiving instruction from God; and if we obey and abide, we can walk forward in His peace and lasting victory. While it takes much less effort to avoid pain, cast blame, attempt control, or talk everyone's ear off about complex feelings, such things do not provide what we need. They are temporary paths of least resistance that lack the wealth required to move us forward. They call us to be obedient to the whims of ourselves and others over God. Worship, quite contrarily, pulls our eyes off our lacking places and needy spaces and sets every preoccupation upon Jesus. True worship is not contingent upon our shifting feelings but bases itself upon the fact that God is worthy, holy, ever-caring, and ever-present at all times. It is taking time to rest in God's presence while stilling the mind, calming the heart, and shifting eyes to the most high God prior to any other reaction taken. It's choosing stillness in the storm.

In short, worship causes our mouths to sing even while undergoing the complexities of great difficulty and sorrow. It is a pause to reorient before moving in any direction. It is waiting for God's guidance through the night. And just as the tree branch creates a bubbling resistance against current, our circumstances can be used to resist former unhealthy patterns so we can sing when storms come. At its heart, the path of least resistance is dull and quiet. I don't know about you, but I would like to create a song, instead.

I am fully convinced I will always face difficulty and loss here on earth, but the times I struggle the most are the times I am lacking intimacy in my relationship with God. I get caught in too many snares when I forgo quiet times of worship and reflection in His presence. When I am slow to worship and too hasty to be still, it is as though I forget those defining words God gave to me. When I am not quiet enough to intimately listen, I do not hear His voice. When I am too selfish to worship Him, my eyes shift and lose focus. Lack of worship directed to God simply means I am worshiping my circumstances instead. If I am not worshiping God, I am worshiping myself and the whims of a temporary world.

I frequently ask God, "How would You like me to worship You?" I often feel unworthy to even step into His presence, as I have nothing to offer Him but my broken self. But He never turns me away. He welcomes me into His chambers time and time again. I am reminded of Psalm 52:17 (NIV) when King David says, *"My sacrifice, O God, is a broken spirit; a broken and contrite heart you, God, will not despise."*

We GET to sing praises to a living God who longs to hear our voices even when (and especially if) we have fallen into pieces. We GET to still our striving before a God who cares about every little portion and each dusty corner of our days. Worshiping Him, in fact, makes us realize it's not at all about us and how broken we are, but how perfectly holy, ridiculously amazing, and wholly satisfying He is. And when we choose to focus on His majesty and exalt Him even amidst imperfect circumstances, we quickly see how the power of pain dilutes in His presence realized. The old hymn sings, "Turn your eyes upon Jesus, look full in His wonderful face, and the things of earth will grow strangely dim in the light of His glory and grace." This is entirely true.

Just as a drop of morning sun tucked inside a raindrop reminds us of how the storms of life do not last forever, the fallen tree humming away in river water shows us how we can sing even though the tragic parts life exist. We can choose to worship while breaking the useless cycles of lesser reactions. We can turn tragedies into songs that would have never existed if grief never came our way. Whether your voice is like a roaring waterfall clamoring with recent loss or a rolling brook of tragic moments long past, sing out. This is worship, too.

when my heart has been made weary
by the cruelty of the temporary
and my hands are emptied
of all traces of strength
when I feel as though
I have nothing to give
and perceive myself unworthy
to receive even a crumb off the floor
You invite me
to recline at Your table
for the most extravagant of feasts

come
crack open the door
of the King's chambers
until it unlatches
even a sliver
then
after feeling
His glowing light
settle warmly upon
wearied skin
watch every lesser desire
slough into the darkness
and with heart fluttering
and curious appetite growing
pull the door
wide open
and fully enter in

Chapter 36

The Joy of Jesus

When I think of worship, I have often attributed it to times of corporate song or somber moments calling for serious reverence and tears. While these hold a place in worship, I have often failed to realize worshiping God reveals the attributes of joy and delight He embodies. Worshiping Him can be so very much *fun*. Resting in Him does not always have to mean being stern and serious, nor is it only bound to song alone. Abiding with Him can reveal how beautifully effervescent His presence is. He is not only capable of taking on every possible burden, but He makes the heart ever so light.

A few months ago, I met with Bev, my spiritual director. She led me in an imaginative exercise in which I was to quiet myself and see how God desired to meet with me. Might I now give a plug for the beauty of imagination? As our days go along, much of our imagination becomes manufactured for us in the form of various entertainment choices. As adults, our imaginations become rusty, intimidating, and less frequented. What was once a place we easily visited as children often becomes an overgrown forest we pass by and refuse to explore. Either that, or we have come to know our imaginations as a place in which we wrestle with sin.

But God created imagination. Every amazing thing you see in this world is a result of His incredible mind. God is not imagined; He owns imagination. He imagined imagination, therefore He can be found and ridiculously enjoyed within our own. I believe our imaginations are not to be reserved for childhood or for sin but to be called upon frequently throughout all our years as a healthy place teeming with wonder. With this in mind, I am quick to engage my imagination because I often find God waiting there for me. Finding Him inside my imagination is not shaping Him into my own image but discovering Him in a place He designed.

"Close your eyes and imagine yourself in a spacious place. What does it look like? What does it feel like?" Bev inquired, without expecting me to verbally respond in the moment. "Imagine Jesus approaching you in this place. He has something to say to you. Listen closely. What might it be?"

With eyes tightly closed, I imagined myself back in Alaska, standing in a Denali National Park valley. Snowcapped mountains surrounded and Denali itself towered in the distance to my right. The atmosphere was still and crisp while skies of cornflower blue stretched above my head. That's when I saw Jesus approaching from the distance, dressed not in a white robe we so often see Him portrayed in paintings, but instead as a common man in winter hiking apparel. However, the smile displayed widely upon His face was anything but common. It was gleaming, and as He drew near, His grin grew even grander. He stopped a few feet in front of me, and the chilly breeze brushed around both of us. He took a deep breath and playfully exclaimed, "YOU'RE IT!" and ran away, laughing. A game of tag with Jesus? Well, alright. This was a first! I ran after Him and caught the back of His shoulder. "You're it!" I yelled. We ran back and forth through the frost-laced meadow as our laughter filled the air.

Soon enough we were both out of breath and stood with our hands on our knees trying to still our racing hearts and catch our shortened breaths. Jesus straightened out His back and stood up tall. Looking all around us, He said to me, "See all of this? This is all for you. I made everything you see, and it's meant to be enjoyed. When you delight in all these things, both big and small, you are worshiping Me. Delighting in what I created for you to enjoy is worship. I don't want you to stay focused on all the things that weigh you down. You're not designed for that. I am full of all the joy you need, and I long to share it with you. And when you are aware of all of this, you bring ME joy. I love to hear about what you're thankful for. I love to see you enjoying the life I gave you. I love when you delight in what I have made. By doing so, you're delighting in Me. By the way, TAG, YOU'RE IT!"

I imagined myself laughing and running with Jesus as though we were two children without a care in the world. When I opened my eyes at Bev's prompting, all I could do was shake my head and smile. Life gets so heavy that at times, I forget Jesus isn't only someone to bring my burdens to as I shower His shoulder with tears, but He is a delightful friend to *enjoy*.

I am getting into the habit of asking myself, "In what ways am I enjoying joy?" Joy is a fruit of the Spirit; it's a characteristic of God. It is a part of His very definition and one of His striking personality traits. Joy is not reserved only for the rich, grief-less, elite, burden-less, or those who seemingly have everything put together. Joy is present in the mess and nestled in the poverty. It's found buried deep in black soil. It's found under the cover of a heavy, charcoal sky. It's there settled in between the worst of the worst and never freezes over in the coldest of days. In other words, wherever Jesus is present, so is joy. And we know there is nowhere His presence does not reach, so it is safe to say His joy is everywhere. Joy does not mean "without great sorrow." It means "great love is present in all things, including sorrow."

Nehemiah 8:10 (NIV) says, *"The joy of the Lord is your strength."* It does not say, "Your own understanding is your strength," nor does it say, "Living a life void of loss is your strength." No, this Scripture passage speaks of the capability of God's striking joy despite trials. It gives us the strength we both crave and require.

During that imaginative exercise with Bev, God spoke through my imagination and painted the most freeing experience. The God who created every atom in the universe wants me to enjoy each one. Not only that, but He wants to enjoy it with me. He longs for me to delight in all of it while experiencing the lightness of His presence. He is not careless or stingy with His joy but generously offers it. His joy is unabashedly and openhandedly extended to all of us at each moment of every day.

Tag, you're it.

How will you begin to accept a greater measure of joy amid your messy, gorgeous days?

joy is not merely discovered
perched upon lofty
mountain tops
but is also stitched
into hidden thickets
along the ascent
and lies in wait
at the very bottom
for those too weary
to even take a step

isn't it something
how we expect God to speak
only using carefully plucked words
from our own language
when, in fact,
the deepest of experiences
do not have words
precise enough to describe them

an embrace
for example
can contain entire stories
without sentences
and the canopy of night
holds galaxies
void of adequate descriptions

perhaps
when we have accused God
of being silent
that is precisely when
He is speaking
the loudest

Chapter 37

Delicate

As the snow softly falls outside our living room window, I notice tiny pieces of art gathering into piles. Glistening in their icy, designer gowns, flake upon flake releases from gray sky. Depending on your view of snow, these cold little wonders can be either a blessing or a curse. They can feel like little bits of magic gifted from winter clouds or like frigid, cruel punishments for choosing to reside someplace subject to the cold.

No matter the view, there is a truth: these delicate flakes are only here for a moment. In fact, the slightest bit of heat applied instantly leads to their demise. Pieces of art here one moment vanish as though they never existed.

The impermanence of this life is similar, I suppose. And I cannot decide, moment to moment, whether it is terribly suffocating or wildly freeing that it is this way. Perhaps it is both at once. I desire for good things to never change because they bring so much joy. The thought of jarring goodbyes makes me feel as though I'm in those deep waters about to run out of air. However, if every wonderful thing stayed, what is this life but a run-on sentence or a song that never ends?

If time moved on and nothing was lost, our lives here would

become this boring, predictable thing. We would forever be stuck at one age, held in the same job, experiencing one kind of weather, and eating the same meals. What if a wedding day never ended? Would it be as special? If we paused our favorite memory and made a home forever inside it, would it still remain our best as it sat unchanging? If this were all true, there would be no new beginnings, no exciting shifting, and no growth or change.

That is why the impermanence of life is, in fact, wildly freeing. Nothing here on earth is fixed into eternal bedrock. Everything here is like snow in the wind, leaves in the breeze, blooms in the heat, and fresh petals of spring. We don't have to labor or tend or grip or control anything because everything around us is transient. In fact, the only certain thing in this life is change. It's complex and simple all at once, isn't it?

The first summer we grew our moonflowers, I was very surprised to learn just how delicate their blooms are. When I reached out to touch the first petal, it reminded me of a snowflake. Obviously, it didn't melt in my hands, but it felt as though it could. The white bloom was thin and delicate like a vapor of breath. If my touch was too harsh, it was sure to ruin or tear. And when Addie came out to smell its fragrance, she giggled at how lightly it tickled her nose with its gentle veins.

I am not sure if it's just our species of moonflower, but each bloom on our vines only opens for one night. The morning following their great starlit debut, they bow their heads and wilt and within a few days slough off as skin. For one, brief, glorious night, each delicate bloom has its time to whisper to the world, "I'm here. It doesn't matter who appreciates or sees, but I'm beautiful as can be right here, right now."

Exhale.

What if instead of feeling suffocated by the impermanence of the world, the delicate nature of this whole life could set us free to love and be loved without restraint, condition, or clause?

What if we could be unafraid of loss? What if we stopped looking to any one person or thing out of need for completion within ourselves? Truth be told, nothing and no one can do such a thing. Only God can.

Right here and right now is delicate. And because it is delicate, it is stunning and remarkable. I appreciate our moonflowers because they are so brief. I have stood outside and stared at them in wonder. I have brought artificial lighting outside in order to capture them on camera during the night. I have smelled their fragrance, ran my fingertips lightly across their petals, and kept track of their blooms. They're here for one magic second of life, and that is precisely why I am so enamored by their existence. It is what makes them so valuable.

Maybe this is why I love music so much, too. It floats through the air—art we can hear and feel but not see and touch. Nobody can catch it, no one can keep it, and it cannot be held in boxes or cages. While song writers claim copyright over tunes, music belongs to every ear who hears it… but only for a moment. The notes are wild things that dance through the air and melt in the breeze. Music is impermanent yet lovely. It spins itself into memory while notes morph and change. It is delicate art. It is free.

In terms of grief and loss, so long as we are alive, we will be well acquainted with the textures they bring. However, they are also delicate—sad songs settling as fog and then pushed along with the wind. Like petals, they will one day fall. Like snow, they will dissipate. But why would we wait for grief to go away to not only see but freely LIVE the beauty and wild value of today? Because this moment, that breath you just took, that minute that just ticked by are gifts, no matter how sad they felt or how complicated they seemed. They are miracles we get to live, and one day everything we know will be entirely changed. Blink. That is how quickly all before your eyes will cease to be.

I hope you won't wait until you feel rested to stay up late and head to the country to stargaze. I hope you don't save burning the best smelling candles and eating the richest cake for "better" days lurking somewhere in the far-off future. I hope you don't wait for the winter to pass to realize there is warmth and color found in every day. I hope you wear the fabulous outfit now, tell your friends and family "I love you" until they grow tired of it, laugh until you cry (even when it is highly inappropriate), and generously give your time, talents, and treasure away like they're all fully stocked in a bursting-at-the-seems storeroom. I hope you don't hold back your love, passion, and creativity because of fear, worry, comparisons, and anxiety. I hope you daringly stare despair in the face and say, "I'm living a beautiful life anyway. In fact, I'm appreciating it so much more because you're a reality." I hope you become free from every shackle that grief attempts to make permanent. Its efforts to do so, after all, are delicate, too.

But you know what's NOT delicate? The human spirit. Nobody can explain what matter it is comprised of. It's something stronger than steel and more immovable than mountains. It is more permanent than bedrock and tougher than concrete. It is certainly more substantial than muscle, determination and tenacity. The human spirit will outlast shifting situations, feelings, eras and endings. It is not forever bound to locations, titles, labels and time. It is eternal. It will transcend this earth with all its frailness. While our bodies will wilt like moonflower petals, our spirits will live forever. The task at hand is this: freely live NOW because this life is so temporary. But also, live with the knowledge that your spirit is not temporary.

While our bodies will wilt like moonflower petals, our souls will live forever. The task at hand is this: freely live NOW because this life is so temporary. But also, live with the knowledge that your soul is *not* temporary. You will end up *somewhere* for all of eternity. Do you know the Lord? Are you living a life overflowing with the truest love in existence—the love that originates from Him? Have you experienced the freedom He freely offers? Have you entrusted your fragile days into His care?

God is far more interested in making you sanctified and holy than He is about your happiness and comfortability. While the trials of this life come because of the limitations sin brought upon this world, Christ followers are never navigating stormy waters alone. *"Peace, be still,"* Jesus said in Mark 4:39 (ESV). One word from His mouth and a new perspective is revealed.

We are permanent spirits living in a delicate world. We are here for a passing moment. Isn't it beautiful? Even with its darkness, ache, complications, and problems, it is quite something. We are travelers and tenders here, not owners.

We do not own music and we cannot make moonflower petals or snowflakes stay. So let's dance and notice and soak in all the sights, scents, textures, and feelings with our spirits tightly woven to the One who created them. We cannot stay here, but while we ARE here, let's live slowly, freely, and unafraid.

Jesus
if a single word
from the expanse
of Your tongue
stills storms
and soothes waves
could You please
recite my name

what if we could hold pain in our palms
like an object we could choose
and while feeling its textures
with tips of fingers
we could peel away
outer layers
exposing the softest gold

we would be fools
to set it down
and wish it away
for this treasure
hidden, laced
and intermingled
must be held, felt
and explored
to be discovered

Chapter 38

He Provides

There are, as always, a litany of things keeping us from the restful enjoyment we were intended to embrace in all seasons. Yes, worry, hurry, pain, abuse, neglect, anxiety, distraction, fear, and loss are found on this list, but so is the constant concern that even after all our striving for a comfortable life, we will somehow be left lacking a certain measure of something we should have. Will we have enough provision for tomorrow? Will our health endure? Will we ever meet the right person to share life with or have children to carry on our legacy? Do we have enough resources to retire in comfort? Will our careers bring in enough income to cover expenses? Will loss claim more of what we have thought to be our own? Will we have enough strength to face difficulty? Goodness, even writing these concerns is quite exhausting.

I am sure most of us have clear memories of the hoarding that occurred during the beginning of the pandemic in 2020. Toilet paper aisles were wiped clean (no pun intended) and grocery stores were like piggy banks someone had tilted upside down and shook the contents from. "There will be a shortage of meat, everyone! Make sure you stock up now!" I heard it declared. In light of this news, many ran to the grocery stores to make sure their freezers could be filled. "Oh wait, now it's canned soup and pasta!" they said. Shelves were then made stark naked because many concerned themselves with their own stock of food at home. Call it fear or name it wisdom, there seems to be an innate need inside many of us to ensure we will not go without.

While I am not trying to shame anyone for caring for themselves and their loved ones, and although I am not trying to persuade you to live in complete irresponsibility, perhaps we could live in a more lasting state of calm if we lived like we believe God is capable of providing everything we need for each situation encountered according to His generous riches. While we are called to generosity and wise stewardship, we are ultimately not the source of even an ounce of our provision. We might often feel (and believe) we are our own providers, but truly, it all comes from Him. We are simply stewards.

I came across lyrics penned by Annie Johnson Flint while I was sitting in front of a crackling fireplace at our local library on a dark, January evening. I had previously learned bits of Annie's story in years past and always felt drawn to her writing. She was orphaned by the age of six and dealt with illness for most of her life, so it is safe to assume she was well acquainted with loss, discomfort, and affliction of various kinds. Nevertheless, she was a fantastic poetess who authored many hope-infused words. This particular hymn of hers that grabbed my attention that night wasn't even published until 1941, several years after she had passed away.

In 1941, the world was entrenched in the Second World War. Difficulty was plentiful. Even though Annie wasn't alive to hear congregations sing the words she wrote, I believe they were pushed out into the world at a perfect time. And while these lyrics have been published in many hymnals since, it is not among the most well-known of old tunes passed down in the church. I am not sure why, because this song contains some of the most beautiful sentences I have ingested outside of Scripture. Annie's hymn entitled "He Giveth More Grace" sings:

> "He giveth more grace as our burdens grow greater,
> He sendeth more strength as our labors increase.
> To added affliction, He addeth His mercy,
> To multiplied trials, He multiplies peace.
> When we have exhausted our store of endurance,
> When our strength has failed ere the day is half done,
> When we reach the end of our hoarded resources
> The Father's full giving has only begun.
> Fear not that thy need shall exceed His provision,
> Our God ever yearns His resources to share.
> Lean hard on the arm everlasting, availing,
> The Father both thee and thy load will upbear.
> His love has no limits, His grace has no measure,
> His power no boundary known unto men.
> For out of His infinite riches in Jesus
> He giveth and giveth and giveth again."

When I first read these words on that cold January day, my eyes kept scanning the line, "Fear not that thy need shall exceed His provision," over and over again. I realized I had been living most of my days fearing that somehow my needs would be greater than what He could provide. Or perhaps I had simply come to believe God did not care enough about the details of my needs. I know in my mind that is not the truth. As a young girl, I had memorized the verse found in Philippians 4:19 (NIV) that says, *"And my God will meet all your needs according to the riches of his glory in Christ Jesus."* I have knowledge He is able, yet my fretting has suggested I do not actually believe it to be true.

Perhaps this is where repentance can play an important

part in resting in who God says He is, because after realizing how limited my faith in His provision I had become, I was compelled to simply call out my disbelief. I dissected it. I laid out all the ways I had tried to control instead of trust. I thought about how ridiculous it is to believe the God of endless resources is incapable of sharing or taking care of our needs. I apologized to God for my brazen disbelief in His goodness and for living with tight fists and closely measured generosity. Is it even called generosity if I scrutinize, weigh, and make certain the gift makes proper sense prior to giving anything away? No, not at all.

Here is another wonderful thing about God: He never belittles us when we come to Him in repentance. He opens His arms up wide, accepts our honesty, wipes our transgressions away, and tosses them as far as the east is from the west (Psalm 103:12). And not only that, if we are open and listening, He shows us how to move forward in new wisdom.

After reading Annie's words, dissecting my disbelief, and repenting, a new thought came into my mind... a thought, I am certain, that came from God and not my own limited intellect. How do I know? His ideas often offend my natural tendencies, while mine exist for my comfort. "What if you generously gave your losses to Me and trusted that I am enough to fill every void left in their wake?" He inquired.

Wait, what?

There, in the middle of that library with Annie's poem in my lap, I contemplated *giving* my losses to God for the very first time. I thought about what it would truly be like to bring all my complex feelings to Him as an offering, and then as a sacrifice. Is it not true, our sorrows build up like layers of ash upon our souls? Or maybe they can be described as the saddest of stories undesirably written into the pages of our own. Painful experiences become a part of us forever, it is true. But it is possible to generously give the *weight* of sorrow and all its complexities back to God. Grief, after all, is the only thing that weighs an incredible amount yet leaves our hands completely empty. My hands are empty, anyhow, so why not give up the weight of something I was not designed to carry around?

Sometimes holding on to pain for prolonged periods of time is appealing, though. Sadness, with its multiple layers of textures and tastes, twists and folds itself all around. Quite frankly, it's easier to stay locked up by its weight. It can even become comfortable to stay this way. We gain attention and pity, we hold valid excuses for poor decisions, and we always have something or someone to blame. Even though it hurts, it's so very easy to remain this way. In a twisted way, pain can become a comfortable place to reside.

However, an absolutely subversive experience would begin to take place if the courage was gathered to say, "God, I give You the weight of my sorrow. I generously give You my losses. I refuse to make my home inside their walls. What would You like to accomplish in me and through me because they took place? You can redeem anything. You can provide everything. You can restore. So would You remake this ache into something beautiful instead?" Courage to say (and genuinely mean) these sentences and questions does not originate from our strength to patch it all together but from our willingness to become reliant on God instead of ourselves.

What if our only rule for living was to allow God to make beauty from rubble? We are not the ones who can make towering works of art from burned down hopes. Such beauty is not contingent on our striving and temporary skills but instead completely dependent on God's stunning capability to create palaces from wreckage with His hands that are infinitely dripping in grace.

"*Lean hard on the arm everlasting, availing; The Father both thee and thy load will upbear.*" Our own arms may fail us, our sorrows may try to drown us and hold us captive, but the Father is the One with us in the deepest depths of suffocating water, wrapping a strong embrace around us while teaching us to relax and breathe. Perhaps this is what giving Him losses and sorrows is like. We still feel the currents of the water. We are still there. We cannot pretend we haven't experienced that which is painful. But He is also there, ever holding us, reminding us we can breathe anywhere if He is present.

I have personally come to realize I cannot fully unfold or restfully relax into this life gifted to me if I despise all the different types of situations that have contributed to my understanding of God and life. Giving my losses back to God has not meant I love walking through dark seasons in life but has instead taught me to look beyond the temporary sting to all the possibilities presenting themselves like sparkling stars peeking through the dead of night. Giving my sorrow to God has meant I am actively choosing to trust that He is more than enough for me, even if everything else is stripped away. It means I have hope.

Loss whispers (or sometimes shouts) into our ears language of "not enough." Such words seep into our souls and leave us believing we are lacking. It tells us to compare our stories to those of others. But the truth is, whether we are married, single, young, old, have ten children, no children, own millions of dollars, or call a meager bank account our own, we all have the exact same thing right here, right now. We have our lives. We have today. We have this breath in our lungs and God's invitation to live life close to His side while holding onto His generous hand. How rich! This is all we need. This is enough. Anything beyond such truths is but a passing breeze. The embellishments, both wonderful and awful, are temporary. Our relationship with God is eternal.

"For out of His infinite riches in Jesus He giveth and giveth and giveth again." Amen.

may I wear smooth the floorboards
leading to Your chambers
as I frequent Your presence, Lord

may my footprints carve
grooves of remembrance
again and again

I want to memorize Your details
while continually discovering
more of who You are

may what I learn of You tomorrow
be even grander
than what I know of You today

perhaps the heart
was never meant to remain
perfectly intact
but to instead
become fractured and broken
until it is supple
and surrendered
and unafraid
of remaining
cracked wide open

Chapter 39

He Restores

"And the God of all grace, who called you to his eternal glory in Christ, after you have suffered a little while, will himself restore you and make you strong, firm and steadfast" (1 Peter 5:10 (NIV).

Have you ever thought about how remarkable it is that a tiny seed carries the past, present, and future inside itself? A moonflower seed exists because there was once flourishing vegetation that led to its creation. There is a seed because there was once a past bloom. As I am writing this in the present, we are in the heart of deep winter and seeds are being stored for safekeeping in containers, cellars, basements, and garages. They are simply existing in rest. Left alone this way, they will only serve as evidence of the past and reality of the present, not a fulfillment of the future purpose waiting under their shells. Without tending, their future will always remain in storage as hope unfulfilled.

However, under the care of the gardener, they will not stay the same. There will be a future even though they seem to be tiny, unassuming freckles in the hand here in the present moment of winter. These seeds have so much potential. What a miracle it is that a small seed created by a past bloom can lead to the most gorgeous towering flower once again. Have you ever *truly* thought about this fascinating wonder? A seed tells the story of days past, exists in the present winter, and hopes for a glorious *restoration* of its true purpose in the future.

Restoration. When I think of this word, my mind often drifts to car restoration, one of Kirk's hobbies. He is one of those people who finds rusty, forgotten vehicles tucked away in weedy junkyards and sees a new world of possibility. The average passerby would leave such heaps of old rubble alone, but to his trained eye, such things can be absolute treasures. Kirk doesn't see these old cars simply in their broken-down state; he perceives potential for restoration. He has romped through tall weeds, taken note of all the possibilities, and backed trailers up to haul old piles of metal into a shop. Through the course of time, and under his knowledgeable supervision, forgotten vehicles coated in rust and decay have slowly transformed into shiny, new, RUNNING machines. They are brought to life before our very eyes. No magic wand is waved to quickly turn rot into automotive royalty. It takes time. And here's another thing: these vehicles never go back to exactly how they were when first assembled in the factory. While they might bear some resemblance of their original state, they are always, ALWAYS a new creation when their restoration process is complete.

When we are in our own processes of restoration, we often expect speed. And not only that, we hope to return to exactly who we were before our point of loss, tragedy, disappointment, and dismay. The truth is, these happenings change us forever. Grief disrupts everything. We can never go back to who we were because we have experienced what we cannot un-live. Some of these things have the potential to send us into our own junkyards of eternal bitter soul-rot because they hurt so badly. Rust forms on all the cracks left in the wake of crushing pain, and soon enough we can find ourselves sitting stuck and broken down in our own tall weeds. We want to be "fixed." We long to go back to how it was. The truth is, we cannot. We cannot properly trailer ourselves out of these junkyards and patch ourselves up. Oh yes, we might try, but self-restoration is not eternal.

Here's the good news: God is incredibly skilled when it comes to His restoration abilities. He sees so much potential in us no matter how we appear to others or what we believe about ourselves. He is the One who can pluck us out of our rotting, and through time, allow us to become remade according to His expertise. It is not so much about fixing what is broken but restoring what has been beaten. It is rarely quick, easy, cheap, or hurried but is instead a slow, gentle process paid for entirely out of the wealth of His generous knowledge and care. He not only knows how to weld pieces together, sew what is split, sandblast, paint, and rebuild, He can create something entirely new from what was once broken down, tired, and seemingly unmendable to the untrained eye. He doesn't dismiss or ignore our pain but helps us use it. He knows how to rename what the enemy has meant for harm. This must be where my friend Beth gleaned her inspiration from in renaming her trials while battling cancer.

Currently, there is a decade standing in between now and the last of our miscarriages, and it has been nineteen years since losing Amy. I can confidently say time does not heal wounds. I still have gashes where it feels as though my heart was ripped out time and time again. We never experienced the arrival of a "rainbow baby" (the term given to children born post-miscarriage) and we never received medical explanations or closure in the natural sense. We still miss Amy every day. I still deeply feel the sorrow and might continue to do so for the rest of my life. In whatever capacity these wounds remain, whether gaping and bleeding, scabbed and healing, or scars forever speaking, they are not minimized in God's presence.

Through time, sorrow has brought opportunities for grace to be amplified in my life. It is as though, when I take Jesus' hand, I feel the stickiness of blood still seeping from where they nailed Him to the cross. I picture Him looking at me, and with all the knowing compassion in the entire universe, He says, "I know it hurts so very much. Let Me walk with you through this ache." If I had never experienced such loss, I would not understand who He is as the restorer of my soul.

As a restorer, God never brings us back to our "factory settings" because He is in the business of making all things new. He considers all we have been through and doesn't write our pain off as unimportant. Instead, He uses it as a base on which to build something entirely new. I am not (and will never again be) who I was prior to loss. Instead, through surrendering, submitting, releasing, enjoying, worshiping, and abiding, I am a new creature. Building upon and not over my wounds, I am continually being remade by the Creator. I am kinder and wiser, and I see things now that my eyes were not previously trained to see. I notice small, passing wonders and sometimes feel gratefulness for every moment so intensely that I barely know how to contain it. I am filled with gritty empathy for others when they experience losses of various kinds and I am unafraid of the darkest of nights. I am quick to hold others' hands while being present with them through ugly situations. I have been there, after all, and I know God is found there, too. There is no night too dark, no loss too great, no pain too complex, no feeling too harsh for God. I know this because I have lived it.

Restoration is unhurried. Just as little seeds must abide all through the dead of winter until the season of brand new, never-before-seen bloom comes, we must be patient, too. It is in the wait we are still enough to become remade. And unlike the restored, gorgeous vehicles that are revealed at the end of their repairing processes, God's restoration occurs in our flesh, bone, hearts, and minds and is never ending here on earth. As long as we are here, we will experience both beauty and ache; but if we are willing, we will constantly be remade by the Restorer of our souls. And one glorious day, when standing in eternity, we will finally be healed and whole. That is when we will be presented as entirely new.

thank You
for all that is difficult
and ugly
all the lacking and aching
and for deeming me
a student of the temporary
so I might recognize
what is worthy of eternity

thank You for my collection of rubble
and ever-changing wounds
for how else
could I know
each and every part
of You?

It is not loss that has given me strength.
Pain has not shaped.
Imperfection has not refined.
There is only one truth that has made me stronger, made life fuller, and brought depth to my days:
God has been present. Near. Abiding. Next to me.
"What doesn't kill you makes you stronger," is a lie, for it is not affliction that births strength.
No, it is only His presence that constructs both armor of strength and coverings of comfort as He enfolds and bestows. It is not about turning pain into strength but allowing His power to be made perfect in weakness.

It is never me.
It is never my pain.
It is never my circumstance.
It is always
only
HIM.

time does not stop
to ask if I have
cherished enough

it does not pause
to make certain
I have enjoyed
all its minutes and days

it does not slow
to look me in the eye
and remind me
it cannot stay

time
is not responsible
for how it is experienced
but confidently
leaves such things
up to you
and up to me

Chapter 40

Though Storms Will Come

On a mid-November morning, my friend Beth called me on the phone with a palpable amount of excitement in her voice. As I stated earlier in "Bloom," Beth was in the throes of her second battle with cancer. In fact, only a month prior to this phone call, she had been given the devastating news that doctors had done all they could. There were no options left, as her cancer had figured its way around every course of treatment regimented.

"Do you have a few moments to chat?" she asked with enthusiasm. Of course, I did. I was curious why Beth sounded so chipper and couldn't wait to find out why. As she dove into her story, goosebumps began to collect on my arms. My friend had experienced an encounter with God, and like any encounter with our Creator, it was quite remarkable.

"Last night I had what I can only explain as an 'experience,'" she explained. "It wasn't a dream, because I got up three times to use the bathroom and get glasses of water, and each time I laid down and closed my eyes, it continued. It didn't feel like a dream. It felt like a vision."

"Go on!" I exclaimed.

"Okay, so I was basically Peter in the boat on that stormy night Jesus walked to the disciples on the water. Except I wasn't Peter, obviously. I was myself. But as Jesus got near to our boat in the middle of that storm, He called out to ME to walk on water to Him. So I did. I got out of the boat and started walking to Jesus. AND SARAH, LET ME TELL YOU, IT WAS SO REAL! I could feel the water heaving beneath my feet. I could feel how unsettled the water was. I could feel the wind in my hair. I could hear the waves crashing all around.

"As I was walking to Jesus, I got scared. Everything was so overwhelming because I couldn't help but pay attention to the storm. It was so loud. And that's when I sank. I went completely under the water and couldn't breathe, so naturally I was terrified. I couldn't see anything because the current was tossing me around. But that's when I felt BOTH of Jesus' arms reach into the water and grab me. He pulled me up to the surface where I was then standing on the water with Him face to face. I could see all the details of Him... it was so real. He was so real! He cupped my face in between both of His hands, looked me in the eye, and said, 'Keep your eyes on Me. Don't focus on the storm surrounding us. Look at Me. I am with you. You may not ever get back on that boat, but even so, will you trust Me?'

"And that's where it ended, but it's like His voice is still echoing in my mind, asking me if I will trust Him even if I never get back on that boat of security and health. I'm definitely not doubting that He can bring healing to my body, but my answer is yes. Even if I'm not healed on this side of heaven, I'm going to keep looking at Him and trusting in Him no matter what's going on in my life. Even if I die from this disease, I'm going to keep trusting Him. How could I not? He even said the storm was surrounding US, not just me. He was there, so really, I didn't have anything to be scared of."

As Beth spoke, I was speechless. In my own humanness, I wanted her back on that boat. I wanted her safe, sound, healed, and far away from the raging seas of cancer. While I rejoiced with her after experiencing such an encounter with God, I didn't want her to leave.

This friend of mine who taught me how to rename the struggles in my life was teaching me another lesson with God's help: God is to be trusted even when all other senses of safety and security are stripped away. He is to be trusted in every storm. He is worthy of this trust as we face the turmoil tucked inside our temporary time here on earth. Even through sickness, hardship, loss, and facing unknown futures, He is our hope. Beth chose to latch on to this even while cancer festered inside her bones.

Eight months later, I took Beth's arm and led her into Kirk's office. She was weak, tired, and nearing the end of her journey. In fact, she had come to talk to us about her funeral. She sensed her remaining time was very short. As she recounted her "experience" walking on the water with Jesus to us, her eyes shone with the same vigor and joy she had the night of her vision.

"I don't want people to be mad at God after I die," she said. "I want them to trust that God knows what He's doing and that this isn't the end. I'm so sad for everyone I'm leaving behind, but I really cannot wait to get to heaven. I'm so excited for what's ahead! He's been with me every step of this storm, and He will see me through its completion."

A couple weeks later, I sat by her bedside and held her hand when it was clear this completion was about to take place. We spoke of heaven and imagined what the food would taste like. I talked with her about my heaven dream... about Amy enjoying the endless buffet of delicious food. We wondered if all our most favorite things would be replaced by even better things in eternity. Yes, we decided, they most certainly will be. We can use up all our words wondering about heaven, but the mysteries that lie there are too wonderful for even the most creative imaginations and grandiose language.

"I'm perfectly peaceful about all of it," she said. "I'm only nervous about the actual moment of dying. Will it hurt? Will it freak me out? I'm not sure. But God is with me, and I'm still trusting Him. I'm not keeping my eyes on the storm. I'm looking at Him."

My eyes welled with tears. I was trying so hard to be brave with her, but my heart was breaking. "Well, just remember time isn't a thing in heaven. Before you know it, you're going to turn around and there we will be with you! You're going to be able to see your loved ones who are there. You'll be able to meet Amy. You'll be able to meet my babies. But even more, you're going to get to look at God face to face! I can't help but be jealous!"

With that, we said we loved each other, and I left to allow her to rest. That would be the last moment I spent with Beth on this side of heaven.

Death is hard to wrap our minds around, isn't it? One day I'm holding Beth's hand, and the next I'm looking at the box containing her ashes. One moment she's here, and the next she is not. The invisible line between here and eternity is but a thin veil. However, she didn't slip through without teaching me a few valuable lessons:

1) Renaming the difficulties in life strips darkness of its power.

Don't call difficulty for what it is only on the surface. Don't allow loss to define who YOU are. Instead of allowing it to define you, rename it. Look past the skin of situations and open your heart to all the possibilities found in the deep.

2) Trusting in God through all the storms of life is the wisest decision we could make.

Trusting in God is wise even if the safety of the boat is never again given to us. Trusting in Him makes sense because He is the only true and lasting giver of peace. He saw Beth through, and He will continue to do the same for all of us.

3) Don't wait to fully appreciate the people and the moments of this wondrous life.

During the days made quiet and slow due to the pandemic shut down, Beth and I would take walks outside together. She was not even a year into her second diagnosis, but I realized how precious and unpromised our time was together. I noticed the way the setting sun caught her hair and turned it into spun gold. I memorized her laugh. I truly listened as she told stories and talked about the details of her day. I felt her hands in mine as we prayed together. I wrote the sound of her voice deep upon my memory. I drank in our moments and savored them because I knew they were precious and fleeting. I realized what we had in those times together was valuable and worth relishing.

One time she said to me, "My friend told me she was trying to memorize all the details of who I am in case I die. I just wish she would appreciate me, and everyone else, with that intensity no matter if we're dying or not. Shouldn't we live that way all the time? We shouldn't ever take each other for granted now." She was so right. All these moments we have—all these breaths we take—are altogether transient. We should not wait to cherish anything. We should do it now.

Beth's cancer journey is over and she has now been transformed into an eternal life spent with Jesus in His kingdom that does not end. Her suffering turned to joy, her trust steadfastly remained, and she is now in perfect rest with her attentive Creator. She never blamed Him for her afflictions because she saw this life for what it is: temporary and subject to imperfections.

Though her absence is felt, I will do as she did and trust God throughout the storms. He is the only One who can bring calm to chaos and order to ruins, and I will always remember her "experience" whenever I'm feeling overwhelmed by the storms surrounding me.

As 2 Corinthians 4:16-18 (NLT) says, *"So no wonder we don't give up. For even though our outer person gradually wears out, our inner being is renewed every single day. We view our slight, short-lived troubles in light of eternity. We see our difficulties as the substance that produces for us an eternal, weighty glory far beyond all comparison, because we don't focus our attention on what is seen but on what is unseen. For what is seen is temporary, but the unseen realm is eternal."*

How can we turn these verses from head knowledge to actual practice, as Beth did? I believe we can by the daily practice of Scripture. We are not to be mere readers of the Word, but doers. James 1:22 (NLT) says, *"But don't just listen to God's word. You must do what it says."* We can choose to view our short-lived troubles in light of eternity. Each loss, grief, and ache of this life truly is so very temporary when perceived through such a lens. There is nothing that won't eventually be made right, even if we cannot understand the process in the present. Times of lightness and joy are so very beautiful, but they add little grit to our faith. It is the long, bleak winters, the surging storms, the stinging winds, and the foggy nights that prove the steadfastness of God's faithfulness. This is what brings forth the substance of our hope and puts our trust into practice.

We can choose to trust and rest hand in hand with Jesus while keeping eyes locked on Him through each loss and every difficulty. We can rename afflictions while weaving our lives tightly around Him. We can live a life of slowing and noticing the details while responding with gratitude and joy even if we must squint to make out the mere shadows of blessing through the foggy night. We can decide to thrive like a beautiful moonflower in the dark seasons of life even when such a thing doesn't make sense in the natural.

We do not have to wait for circumstances to fall into ideal order to truly live; we are invited to fully breathe right here, right now, no matter what. Even in the deep waters, and even in the night. Life is this gorgeous thing even when it hurts. We can choose to live out this belief not in our own strength alone but with His realized nearness right next to us with every step. Out of all the things we must let go of, God is the one and only thing we will never have to bid goodbye. And of them all, He is the very best. In actuality, we are so very rich through both life and death because the richest part of our whole existence—the nearness of God—is incapable of being lost on those who love Him.

As for me, I have decided to practice this belief daily even when it is insanely difficult. I have now chosen to ditch the "perfect pastor" persona that nobody besides myself ever demanded I wear. I have decided to be wisely transparent and honestly vulnerable because that is where I have found a much greater measure of health and freedom. I have been terribly broken by grief, loss, and pain, but I have also bloomed despite all of it. And Christ, in His gentle nearness, is constantly teaching me there is so much lying beyond what I can hold and see in the here and now.

And as for our five children who are in heaven, their beautiful lives are anything but a waste. The worship song "Graves into Gardens"[1] includes the lyrics, *"You turn graves into gardens, You turn bones into armies... You're the only One who can."* These words have taken on such a personal meaning to me because God is the only One who could turn the graves of our children into a garden that sings of His faithfulness found inside the grief. He is the only One capable of turning death into the most vibrant life. He alone scatters these ashes of sorrow into the night sky, illuminates them like shining stars, and creates the most beautiful landscapes from rubble. In fact, our five are like a tiny army who will always champion the truth of God's goodness. As long as I am alive, they will forever help me speak, sing, shout, and proclaim God's goodness that is found in the darkest of nights. One day, I will hold them in my arms, but for now, they are the most vibrant flowers rising next to me in an evening garden planted under the most gorgeous, glittery sky.

Chapter 41

An Invitation

And so the moonflower seeds are scooped from their rest by the tender hand of the Great Gardener. Fresh soil has been prepared, and spring has arrived with its new, glorious promise of life. It is time for breaking, soaking, and pressing into the earth. Vines will climb and petals will unfold under a velvety, star-speckled night sky. They will rebelliously thrive under the cover of evening tide just as they were intended. This is what the moonflowers are known for, after all.

For the rest of my days, I will do the same.

And the same invitation is open to you.

No matter the darkness, we can thrive here, too.

"Those who sow with tears will reap with songs of joy. Those who go out weeping, carrying seed to sow, will return with songs of joy, carrying sheaves with them." Psalm 126:5-6 (NIV)

does anything
truly end
or is it simply
a continual
unfolding

Acknowledgments

Books, I have learned, do not magically appear, and authors need a great deal of support to bring their words life. I am no exception. While reading this book, you're not only reading my voice but that of so many others who have helped and encouraged me through its lengthy shaping. *Moonflower* would not exist without such wonderful people.

First and foremost, so much gratitude to my husband, Kirk. You have been my greatest source of long-standing, steadfast encouragement and support. This story is as much yours as it is mine, and it is you who kept me going when I wanted to burn it all to the ground several times over. You're one of the most humble and talented people I have the honor of knowing and loving, and your wisdom has been, and will continue to be, my north star. You have lived through tragedies by my side and have taught me how to trust in God through it all. You're my most favorite.

Our dear Addie—what a dazzling light you are in our lives. I hope you always know you are miraculous, brilliant, and completely delightful. You, without a doubt, are supposed to be here, and watching you grow into a young woman has been the honor of my life. Every part of your character amazes me, and I cannot believe God chose you—the sweetest of daughters—to be ours. As Ecclesiastes 4:12 says, "*A cord of three strands is not quickly broken.*" You, your father, and I are braided together. *Moonflower* is your story, too.

Dan Herod—you were among the first to give encouragement and helpful insight as I began to write. I will never forget you saying, "When you're writing, picture your readers holding your book. Speak to them directly. They need to hear your words. Keep going." Your early expertise kept me authentic and your words reverberated in my mind as every sentence was typed.

Bev—as my spiritual director, you are also one of my pastors. Thank you for teaching me to keep my imagination fresh and biblically rooted, as it is in this combination I have come to develop such an intimate relationship with Jesus. You have cared for me so well through the years, and your encouragement while authoring has been invaluable!

To my dear friends and family who have been among my early readers throughout the writing process, giving me pointers and helping me rephrase and rearrange—Ron, Lynda, Aaron, May, Cindi, Andrea, Bethany, Ashley, Ashlee, Curtis, Alyssa, Julie, Marni, and of course my mom (who read several versions of *Moonflower* throughout the last three years). Thank you for taking the time to make sure I wasn't trying to write in a voice contrary to my own. You kept me well rooted throughout the writing process.

Emily Person, what an honor it is to have your artwork on the cover and in the pages of *Moonflower*. Ever since I found your work in *Every Moment Holy, Volume III*, I felt drawn to your talent. I am still in awe of how perfectly you brought my vision to life. As an "unknown author," you made me feel seen and worth your time. I will forever be grateful!

To Nick Poe of Tall Pine Books—thank you for offering a welcoming, loving space in which to plant *Moonflower*. God clearly led me to you just as I was releasing expectations of how I thought this publishing process would go. The care and personalization you have exemplified has brought so much peace.

Moonflower did not find its beginnings in a book deal with a big-box publisher, nor amidst agent representation or advocacy. Instead, it began in the quietest, most personalized of ways. I will never forget Thursday, May 30th, 2024—the night my community gathered to share music, art, dance, and poetry to raise funds for this book to exist. It was as though the hands of my loved ones sowed the seed of this book together, collectively pressing it into the dirt so it could have a chance to bloom. *Moonflower* exists because of all their generosity and love. There is no better way, in my opinion, for this book to have found its start. It is going out into the world not as a shout but as a whisper rooted in deep love.

Dear reader, I am also grateful for you. I have been praying for you for years. As each word was typed, you were on my mind. I have no social platform on which to stand, and this book has been so quietly released, so the mere chance you met the words on these pages is miraculous in and of itself. I have asked God to give this book legs and wings to find its way into your hands. I truly pray you would come to know Jesus in such sweet, personal ways and that you would allow Him to become the pillar of support you lean upon when waves of difficulty come. I hope you felt cared for and "at home" within these pages.

Above all and higher than any other, I am thankful for God, the author of my story. From Him, for Him, and to Him alone I give my whole life as a broken and poured-out offering. Through everything great and terrible, wonderful and awful, He has proven to be steadfast, faithful and worthy of all of my deepest adoration and affection. Through every loss, He is constant. He is my keeper, sustainer, and the lifter of my head. *Moonflower* is for His glory alone.

Discussion Questions

Chapter One: Am I Drowning, or Am I Breathing?

1. The author and her daughter experience identical dreams that lead them to a deeper understanding of their relationship with God. How do you think shared experiences, whether in dreams or real-life events, contribute to spiritual growth and understanding? How might this idea be applied to community or family settings?
2. The chapter describes a dream where the author and her daughter are submerged in water, initially feeling fear but eventually finding peace as they learn to breathe underwater. What might the water symbolize in this context, and how does it relate to the idea of faith and trust in God when facing the unknown or difficult situations in life?

Discussion Questions

Chapter Two: Broken Open

1. The chapter uses the metaphor of a moonflower seed being pierced and soaked before it can grow to describe a deeply painful experience. How does this metaphor relate to the author's experience of loss, and what insights can it offer about the purpose or value of suffering in personal growth and healing?
2. The author struggles to reconcile her role as a worship leader with the pain of losing a child, questioning God's goodness in the process. How does this conflict highlight the challenges of maintaining faith during times of profound grief? How might these challenges influence a person's relationship with God and their community?

Chapter Three: Again and Again and Again

1. In this chapter, the author reflects on the experience of losing multiple pregnancies despite having strong faith and praying fervently. How does this challenge the conventional understanding of faith as something that can control outcomes? What does this suggest about the nature of faith when prayers go unanswered, and how might it shape a person's spiritual journey?
2. The chapter addresses the misconception that tragedy occurs due to a lack of faith. How can this belief be harmful, both to individuals experiencing loss and to the broader community? What alternative understanding of faith does the author propose, and how might this perspective help people navigate difficult circumstances?

Chapter Four: After

1. Here we have a section that vividly describes the emotional aftermath of miscarriage, including feelings of guilt, loneliness, and the struggle to find closure. How do these experiences highlight the unique nature of grief associated with miscarriage compared to other forms of loss? What insights can be drawn about the long-term impact of this grief on a person's mental and emotional well-being?
2. The chapter touches on how others' responses to miscarriage, though often well-intentioned, can sometimes be hurtful or confusing. How can this affect the grieving process for someone who has experienced miscarriage? What might this suggest about the importance of thoughtful and sensitive support from friends, family, and the broader community in helping someone navigate such a loss?

Chapter Five: The Shadow Place

1. Reflect on the presence of God in the midst of suffering and grief. The chapter describes the author's profound pain following multiple miscarriages and the eventual sense of God's presence in her darkest moments. How does this experience challenge common perceptions of how God interacts with us during times of intense sorrow? What insights does this offer about the nature of God's comfort and presence, even when our circumstances do not change?

DISCUSSION QUESTIONS

2. The author describes how her expectations of life and faith were shattered by repeated losses, leading to a deeper understanding that the temporary world cannot offer what is only found in eternity. How does this realization reshape the way we approach life's hardships and our relationship with God? In what ways can adjusting our expectations help us find peace and resilience in the face of ongoing trials?

CHAPTER SIX: HIS HAND

1. Many attempt to find healing through books, programs, and advice, only to discover that these man-made solutions often fall short. How does this realization shape our understanding of the grieving process? What does this suggest about the role of faith and the presence of God in finding true healing and transformation amidst deep sorrow?
2. In the chapter, the author experiences a vision of Jesus walking with her through darkness, offering assurance through His laughter and presence. In what ways does this experience challenge or reinforce the author's decision to trust in God, even when His presence feels distant or His plans are unclear? How can experiences with God impact us compared to merely knowing *about* God?

CHAPTER SEVEN: SILENCING WHY

1. Explore the role of unanswered questions in the journey of faith. The chapter discusses the persistent question of "why" in the face of loss and

how it often leads to frustration and a lack of fulfillment. How does the decision to release the need for answers and instead focus on trust in God change the dynamic of the our relationship with God? What can this teach us about the nature of faith when faced with life's most difficult and unanswerable questions?
2. Reflect on the shift from seeking answers to seeking presence. How does this shift in focus impact the healing process? What does this suggest about the potential benefits of moving from a posture of questioning to one of surrender and trust in the midst of suffering?

Chapter Eight: Loss is Loss is Loss

1. Discuss the dangers of comparing pain and grief. How does the act of comparing pain and grief create barriers to healing and connection? What can this teach us about the importance of empathy and support in the face of different types of loss?
2. The chapter emphasizes the idea that grief is a universal experience that should not be ranked or compared but rather shared and supported. How can embracing this perspective foster a deeper sense of community and mutual understanding? In what ways might sitting together in grief, without trying to categorize or diminish it, lead to collective healing and growth?

Discussion Questions

Chapter Nine: Frostbitten

1. The chapter draws a parallel between the need to protect vulnerable plants from frost and the need for God's covering to protect us from life's difficulties. How does the author describe the role of God's presence and protection in helping us endure and grow despite challenging circumstances? What can this teach us about the importance of cultivating a deep relationship with God as a source of strength and refuge?
2. Reflect on the importance of attentiveness in spiritual growth. The chapter mentions how the failure to protect the garden from frost led to the loss of some plants, emphasizing the need for vigilance. How does this metaphor relate to our spiritual lives, particularly in terms of being attentive to potential threats to our growth and well-being? What practices or habits can help us remain alert and responsive to the spiritual "frosts" that may come our way?

Chapter Ten: The Patient Gardener

1. Our spiritual growth is compared to the process of a seed being planted and tended by a gardener. How can trusting in God's wisdom and timing, even when the process is uncomfortable or different from what we expected, impact our spiritual growth? What are some practical ways to cultivate this trust in your daily life?
2. The chapter emphasizes that, unlike actual seeds, we have a choice in whether or not we thrive in the

Discussion Questions

environment God has provided. How can you actively participate in your spiritual growth, especially when faced with challenges or discomfort? What practices can help you remain open to God's nurturing and avoid becoming "stalled out" in fertile soil?

Chapter Eleven: Spring Always Comes

1. How does the metaphor of *delayed spring* relate to seasons of grief and waiting? How can recognizing that "spring always comes" help us maintain hope and patience during prolonged periods of hardship or loss? What practical steps can you take to remind yourself of this truth when you feel stuck in a "winter" season?
2. Examine the role of God's unchanging nature in the midst of changing circumstances. What are some biblical instances of God remaining steadfast in the face of changing circumstances? How can you allow these examples to fuel your own endurance?

Chapter Twelve: Pressed Down

1. Reflect on the choices we face in times of deep pain and darkness. What is the short term and long term ramification of allowing wounds to dominate our growth process?
2. Deuteronomy 31:8 states, "The Lord himself goes before you and will be with you; he will never leave you nor forsake you. Do not be afraid; do not be discouraged." How can this promise of God's unwavering presence and guidance provide comfort

DISCUSSION QUESTIONS

and strength during seasons of pain and uncertainty? In what ways can this verse encourage you to trust in God's plan, even when you are in the midst of "darkened dirt" and cannot see what lies ahead?

CHAPTER THIRTEEN: SOFT AND SLOW

1. Reflect on the role of gratitude in the healing process. How can actively practicing gratitude help shift your focus from the pain and challenges in your life to the hidden blessings and growth opportunities? What are some practical ways to incorporate gratitude into your daily routine?
2. Examine the significance of paying attention to life's subtle transitions. How can becoming more mindful of the small, often overlooked transitions in your own life help you recognize and appreciate the gradual growth and healing taking place? In what ways can slowing down and noticing these details enhance your overall sense of well-being and connection to the present moment?

CHAPTER FOURTEEN: TEARS

1. It's important to allow yourself to feel emotions as part of the healing process. How can giving yourself permission to feel and release emotions, rather than suppressing them, contribute to your emotional and spiritual well-being? What are the pitfalls of refusing to allow yourself to *feel*?
2. The author describes how God is a compassionate and understanding presence who welcomes our

tears and emotions without judgment. How does viewing God as a safe space for your emotions change the way you approach Him in prayer and worship? In what ways can you deepen your relationship with God by being more transparent and vulnerable about your feelings?

Chapter Fifteen: Amber Gems

1. Consider the coexistence of pain and hope in your life. How can recognizing the presence of hope *within* your pain change your perspective on difficult experiences? What practices or habits can help you actively search for and appreciate the "diamonds of hope" in the midst of life's storms?
2. What are some biblical examples of pain and hope coexisting at once? What truths can be gathered from these examples? Do you have past experience with these realities in your own personal history with God?

Chapter Sixteen: The Power of a Name

1. In the chapter Beth renamed her chemotherapy treatment from "Red Devil" to "Rose," transforming her mindset and opening up opportunities for hope and gratitude. How can renaming your struggles or challenges help shift your focus from pain to potential blessings? What are some specific challenges in your life that you could rename, and how might this change your perspective on those situations?

DISCUSSION QUESTIONS

2. Have you under appreciated the power and impact of a name? Are there other ways you have allowed a name to dictate how you see situations, for better or worse?

CHAPTER SEVENTEEN: POISON IN THE BONES

1. The chapter highlights how the author learned to find beauty and joy in life even while carrying the pain of loss, similar to how the moonflower blooms despite containing poison. How can acknowledging and embracing both the joy and pain in your life lead to a more profound and authentic experience of living? What are some of the "poisons" in your life that you can bloom in the midst of?
2. The author describes a significant change in perspective when she shifted her prayers from asking for more to appreciating what she already had. How can this shift in focus from what is missing in your life to what is currently present enhance your sense of gratitude and contentment? What steps can you take to cultivate this mindset daily, and how might it help you discover hidden joys and opportunities for growth that you might otherwise overlook?

CHAPTER EIGHTEEN: AND SHE HEARD THE BIRDS

1. The chapter highlights how Amy found redemption in noticing and appreciating the birds after her mother's passing, something she had previously dismissed. What are some areas in your life where you might have overlooked small, meaningful

Discussion Questions

details or taken relationships for granted? How can you seek and embrace opportunities for redemption in these areas, even after experiencing loss or regret?
2. How can you make a conscious effort to fully engage in conversations with the people you care about, especially in moments that might seem mundane, this week? How can these practices heighten and strengthen our peace and contentment?

Chapter Nineteen: Songs of Deliverance

1. Taking slow, intentional walks to connect with God and notice the details of His creation is very important. How can you incorporate a similar practice into your routine, allowing yourself time to walk with Jesus and listen for His voice? What changes might you need to make in your schedule or mindset to prioritize this form of spiritual exercise, and how do you think it could impact your relationship with God?
2. Think about the significance of experiencing God's presence in everyday moments. How can you cultivate an awareness of God's presence in your own life, especially during ordinary activities like walking, working, or resting? What steps can you take to remind yourself of His constant companionship and to respond to His invitations for deeper connection throughout your day?

Chapter Twenty: Upward

1. The chapter compares Jesus to a trellis that supports and sustains growth, emphasizing that apart from

Discussion Questions

Him, we cannot flourish as intended. How does being "grafted" into Jesus' truth, rather than relying on your own, influence your spiritual growth and ability to endure difficult seasons? Can you think of any cautionary tales in your life or the life of someone else that stems from ignoring this grafting process?

2. There are serious limitations and pitfalls of living according to personal truths, which are often self-centered and temporary. How has relying on your own truth led to challenges or dissatisfaction in your life? What can you do to replace self-centered truths with the enduring and life-giving truth of God, and how might this shift impact your perspective on life and your relationship with Him?

Chapter Twenty-One: But Now I See

1. Loss can act as a lens, bringing clarity and a deeper appreciation for the small details of life. How has experiencing loss or hardship in your own life changed the way you perceive the world around you? What specific moments or details have you begun to notice and appreciate more since going through that experience?

2. The author describes a slow change in her eye sight that happened over time. Can our spiritual vision slowly become worse over time, even without our noticing? How can we take inventory of this and take steps to clear up what we are seeing, spiritually speaking?

Discussion Questions

Chapter Twenty-Two: Unearthing Treasure

1. Take time to observe something in nature or in yourself that you may have overlooked before—how does this change your perspective on God's craftsmanship and attentiveness? What are the pitfalls of living too quickly, without stopping to notice subtle beauty?
2. Here the author reflects on the tendency to focus on perceived flaws rather than embracing the unique aspects of God's creation in ourselves. How can Psalm 139:13-18 challenge and change your view of your own self-worth and uniqueness? What steps can you take to shift your focus from self-criticism to gratitude for the way God has uniquely designed you?

Chapter Twenty-Three: Pruning

1. In John 15:1-3, Jesus speaks of God as the gardener who prunes fruitful branches so they will bear even more fruit. What areas of your life might God be seeking to prune in order to promote greater spiritual growth? Take time to reflect on any habits, attitudes, or even "good" activities that might be hindering your relationship with God. How can you actively surrender these areas to His care?
2. Pruning is described as a holy but often uncomfortable process. How have you experienced God's pruning in your life? Consider a time when God removed something from your life that was initially difficult to let go of. How did that

DISCUSSION QUESTIONS

experience ultimately lead to spiritual growth or deeper understanding?

Chapter Twenty-Four: Release

1. Endings, like autumn and sunsets, symbolize not just closure but also the beginning of something new. Think about a recent or current season in your life that feels like an ending. How can you reframe this experience as a *transition* rather than a *conclusion*? What new beginnings might God be preparing for you through this season of change?
2. Surrender is described as a painful yet necessary act that leads to new life. What areas of your life are you holding onto tightly, resisting the process of surrender? How might releasing control and trusting God in these areas open the door to new growth and deeper spiritual freedom?

Chapter Twenty-Five: Open Hands

1. How can the teachings of Jesus that relate to surrender in Luke 12:22-34 bring more freedom, peace, and trust in God's provision? What does this section of scripture teach you about the heart of the Father?
2. Oma's life is described as a collection of psalms, demonstrating a legacy of faith, trust, and surrender to God. What kind of legacy are you building through your own life experiences, actions, and attitudes? How can you start or continue to cultivate a legacy that reflects a deep trust in God, even through life's challenges and losses?

Discussion Questions

Chapter Twenty-Six: Surrender and Submission

1. As it pertains to surrender and submission, the chapter notes that, "...First, there must be a ceasing of resistance. Then, there must be a yielding to an authority that is not ours." Practically speaking, what do these two steps look like in our Christian walk?
2. The chapter prescribes fixing our eyes on *eternity*. What are the consequences of setting our eyes on temporary things and ignoring the eternal? What are some examples of this?

Chapter Twenty-Seven: Amy

1. What can you learn from Amy's example about surrendering your fears and doubts to God, especially when the future is unclear? How might embracing this type of faith impact your current circumstances?
2. The chapter discusses the concept of viewing death not as an end but as a transition to eternal life, where pain and suffering no longer exist. How does this eternal perspective change the way you view your current struggles and losses? What are a few direct results of losing your fear of death?

Chapter Twenty-Eight: A Gift

1. The dream described in the chapter offers a glimpse into the beauty and joy of heaven, where earthly trials and sorrows are replaced with eternal life in

Discussion Questions

God's presence. How does the promise of heaven impact your perspective on the challenges and losses you face in your life? In what ways can focusing on the hope of eternity with God help you navigate difficult situations with greater faith and peace?

2. The author states, "All these endings we have faced will be redeemed beyond our wildest dreams." What does this say about the love of Jesus toward us? What questions do you look forward to asking one day in heaven?

Chapter Twenty-Nine: Fear and Anxiety

1. Reflect on the moments in your life when fear and anxiety have taken hold. What specific situations or thoughts trigger these feelings for you? How do these experiences reveal areas where you might struggle to fully trust in God's goodness and sovereignty? Consider how you can bring these specific fears and anxieties before God, seeking His healing and peace.
2. We are called to wear God's presence as a garment of protection against fear and anxiety. How can you practically incorporate this idea into your daily life? What is God's perspective toward anxiety and how can you adopt it?

Chapter Thirty: Let Go

1. We should not being anxious over what we cannot control. What are some things in your life that you

can control? What is the impact of fretting over things we cannot control?
2. The chapter ends with a powerful affirmation of being seen, known, and loved by God. How can you cultivate a deeper awareness of God's presence in your life, especially during moments of doubt or feelings of worthlessness? In what ways can you remind yourself daily that you are deeply loved and that His adoring gaze is always upon you?

Chapter Thirty-One: Dancing in October

1. The chapter beautifully illustrates the concept of surrender through the metaphor of autumn leaves letting go. How can you extend this metaphor in your spiritual life? How can you live with joy through various cycles and season of life?
2. Surrendering to God is not a loss but a beautiful act of trust that leads to renewal and peace. Failing to surrender *is* a loss. But why? How does a failure to surrender lead to loss and hurt? Recall specific instances of this.

Chapter Thirty-Two: Rest is Surely Coming

1. How can you prepare for a season of rest or renewal? What does it look like to be ready to recuperate and renew?
2. The chapter notes, "Gardeners do not grow vegetables without the end goal of harvest." Are we guilty of sometimes forgetting the end goal of blessings in our lives? How can we recalibrate our thinking in this way?

Discussion Questions

Chapter Thirty-Three: Joy Remains

1. The chapter describes how a shift in perspective allowed for the discovery of joy in a season that was previously dreaded. Reflect on a season in your life that you initially resisted or disliked. What steps can you take to shift your perspective and find joy in the midst of challenging or uncomfortable circumstances? How can you invite God into that process to help you uncover hidden blessings?
2. The author mentions the importance of not wasting days by merely surviving them, but instead embracing them with joy. How can you apply this mindset to your daily life, especially in seasons that feel difficult or barren? What are the effects of failing to do so?

Chapter Thirty-Four: Abide

1. How much time do you intentionally set aside for rest and to abide with God? What are some specific and real-world benefits of prioritizing this time?
2. The author discusses how societal pressures and personal expectations often lead to a constant state of "doing" rather than "being." How do you currently define success in your life? How might embracing a perspective of "being" rather than "doing" alter your understanding of success?

Discussion Questions

Chapter Thirty-Five: This is Worship, Too

1. How might incorporating worship as a first response have impact on your negative experiences? How can you integrate worship more intentionally into your life? Based on the Psalms and stories of the life of David, what do you suppose he would have to say regarding the value of worship in his life?
2. The author contrasts the habitual, knee-jerk reactions to pain—like avoidance, blame, or seeking control—with the choice to worship, which shifts focus to God. Consider your own patterns of reaction when confronted with difficulties. What unhealthy cycles do you find yourself caught in in these settings? How might choosing worship as a response help you break these cycles and lead to lasting peace and growth?

Chapter Thirty-Six: The Joy of Jesus

1. The chapter points to a powerful experience of using imagination to connect with God and discover the joy in His presence. Reflect on a time when you felt distant from joy in your relationship with God. How might engaging your imagination, as the author did, help you reconnect with the joy and delight that God offers?
2. Nehemiah 8:10 states, "The joy of the Lord is your strength." Consider how this verse applies to your own life, especially during difficult times. How has God's joy provided strength for you in the past, or how might it do so in the future? Is joy a feeling, a

DISCUSSION QUESTIONS

state of mind, or an actual tangible force from God? Or all of the above?

CHAPTER THIRTY-SEVEN: DELICATE

1. Here the author reflects on the delicate and transient nature of life, comparing it to the fleeting beauty of snowflakes and moonflowers. How does recognizing the impermanence of life influence your perspective on the present moment? In what ways can acknowledging the temporary nature of your experiences lead to a deeper appreciation for the beauty and value of each day?
2. Your soul will outlast your earthly experiences. How does this shape your priorities and decisions? In what ways can you align your daily life with the eternal perspective the author encourages, living freely and unafraid while staying connected to the Creator?

CHAPTER THIRTY-EIGHT: HE PROVIDES

1. How does the hymn "He Giveth More Grace" challenge your perceptions of God's provision? Reflect on the line, "Fear not that thy need shall exceed His provision," and discuss how this belief could change the way you approach daily challenges and uncertainties.
2. The author describes the act of giving losses and sorrows to God as a transformative process that allows for healing and the creation of beauty from pain. How do you currently handle grief and loss in your life? What does it mean to "generously give

your losses to God," and how might this practice influence your healing process?

Chapter Thirty-Nine: He Restores

1. This chapter compares the process of spiritual restoration to the restoration of old vehicles, emphasizing that it's a slow, deliberate process that doesn't return us to our "factory settings" but instead creates something entirely new. Reflect on a time in your life when you experienced a significant loss or setback. How has God been at work in your life since then, not merely "fixing" you but transforming you into something new? How does this understanding of restoration change your perspective on suffering and personal growth?
2. Patience in the process of restoration is critical. In what areas of your life do you struggle with impatience, especially when waiting for healing or change? How can you cultivate a spirit of patience, trusting that God is at work even when you can't see immediate results?

Chapter Forty: Though Storms Will Come

1. Beth's vision and her steadfast trust in God, even when facing the reality of her illness, demonstrate a profound faith. Reflect on a time in your life when you were facing a "storm." How did you respond to it? Did you find it challenging to trust God during that time? Recall those key promises, scriptures, prayers, songs, or words of encouragement that helped you through.

DISCUSSION QUESTIONS

2. The author reflects that she has ditched the "perfect pastor" persona that nobody besides herself ever demanded she wear. What are some personas that you have adopted knowingly or unknowingly? Have you put self-inflicted pressure into your own life? How can you remedy this and step into the freedom and healing that Jesus paid for?

About the Author

Sarah Beth Gerbers is a creative arts pastor at Destiny Church in De Pere, Wisconsin. She has a passion for teaching others how to flourish through various art forms and has been in ministry for over two decades. Her husband Kirk and daughter Addie are her most favorite people, and she loves oil painting, writing music and reading through stacks of beloved books.

Notes

17. Poison in the Bones

1. https://leafyjournal.com/are-moonflowers-poisonous/

23. Pruning

1. https://www.gardeningknowhow.com/ornamental/vines/moonflower/cutting-back-moonflowers.htm

29. Fear and Anxiety

1. https://www.nami.org/About-Mental-Illness/Mental-Health-Conditions/Anxiety-Disorders

40. Though Storms Will Come

1. "Graves into Gardens" by Brandon Lake, Chris Brown, Steven Furtick, and Tiffany Hammer

Index

A
    anxiety, anxious · 76, 136, 183, 180, 181, 182, 184, 185, 186, 187, 188, 189, 190, 191, 201, 238, 244, 295

B
    Bible, biblical · 2, 26, 32, 94, 92, 152, 154, 211

C
    childhood · 213, 228
    community · 175, 272, 274, 272, 274, 278

D
    Deliverance · II, III, 287
    depression · 12, 60

E
    eternity, eternal · 25, 26, 32, 144, 154, 160, 165, 167, 170, 175, 177, 179, 182, 238, 256, 257, 260, 262, 264, 276, 293, 295

INDEX

F

fear · 12, 47, 52, 80, 82, 158, 179, 183, 180, 181, 182, 184, 185, 186, 188, 190, 191, 194, 201, 238, 244, 242, 274, 293, 295
forgive · 147
freedom · 119, 144, 146, 239, 266, 291, 305

G

grace · 243, 301
grief · 32, 44, 120, 124, 247, 250

H

Holy Spirit · 30, 35

I

invest · 59

K

Kingdom · 148

L

love · 4, 7, 47, 44, 46, 79, 92, 105, 113, 117, 119, 121, 127, 147, 148, 152, 153, 162, 167, 169, 172, 175, 182, 211, 215, 222, 229, 230, 234, 236, 238, 243, 249, 266, 272, 295

M

memory
memories · 32, 44, 60, 80, 87, 125, 172, 173, 211, 234, 236, 263
mind · 3, 26, 32, 46, 74, 80, 94, 100, 106, 118, 124, 125, 138, 154, 152, 158, 167, 169, 173, 171, 179, 183, 180, 201, 213, 211, 221, 228, 243, 245, 250, 258, 271, 272, 301

P

pain · 5, 11, 28, 30, 34, 32, 33, 35, 37, 44, 46, 57, 61, 64, 67, 74, 76, 80, 82, 84, 86, 95, 102, 120, 132, 146, 152, 160, 163, 165, 167, 177, 215,

221, 223, 242, 244, 247, 251, 252, 254, 258, 266, 272, 274, 278, 280, 281, 283, 285, 293, 299, 301

    prayer, pray · 27, 44, 92, 175, 215, 283

S

    salvation, save · 19

    sin · 44, 52, 160, 181, 194, 228, 240

    sorrow · 12, 17, 19, 30, 32, 44, 64, 74, 98, 108, 109, 122, 173, 221, 230, 245, 247, 249, 252, 254, 267, 274, 276

    soul · 4, 5, 15, 12, 25, 38, 39, 46, 62, 63, 113, 115, 119, 129, 188, 195, 218, 238, 251, 254, 301

    surrender · 5, 136, 138, 143, 144, 152, 154, 152, 154, 155, 156, 158, 160, 165, 167, 169, 179, 182, 188, 189, 198, 199, 201, 206, 254, 278, 290, 291, 293, 297

T

    test, tested · 15, 29

    trauma · 30

U

    understanding · 42, 129, 146, 147, 179, 230, 274, 272, 273, 276, 278, 282, 291, 298, 303

V

    value · 14, 9, 99, 102, 106, 119, 129, 154, 156, 236, 272, 299, 301

W

    wisdom · 15, 50, 95, 147, 146, 148, 150, 152, 162, 201, 242, 245, 270, 279